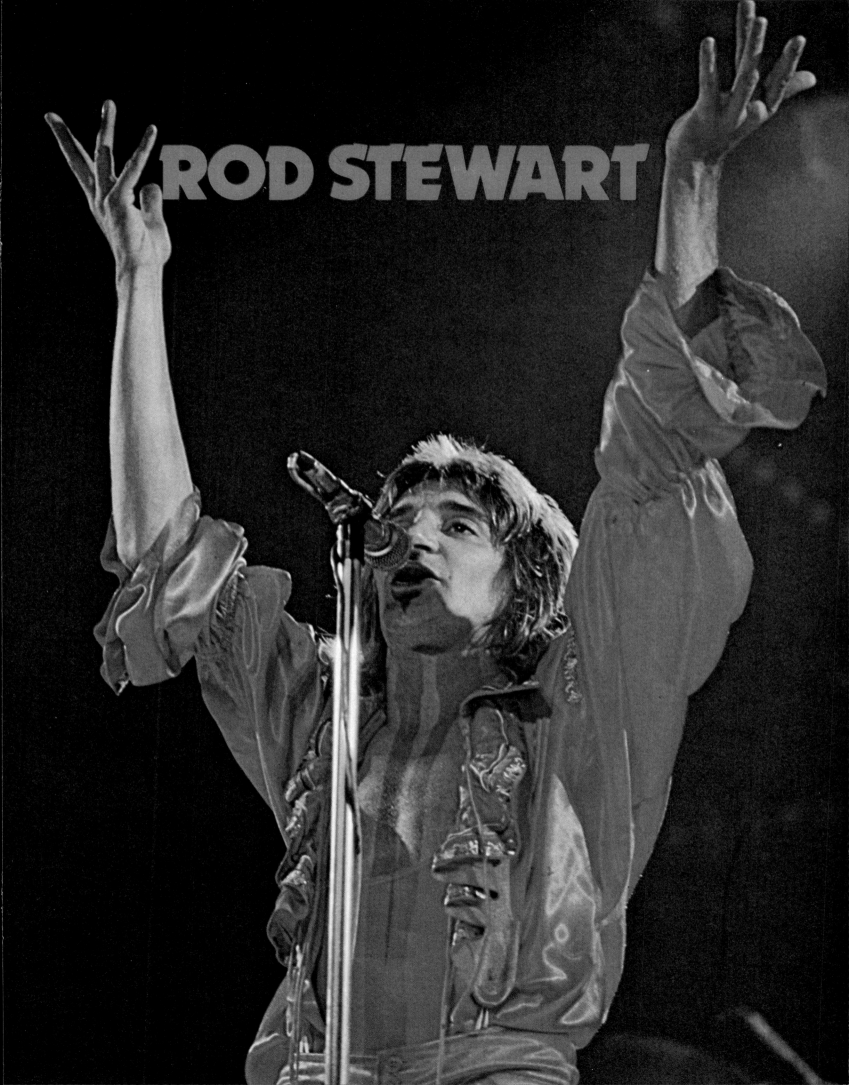

ROD STEWART

Tony Jasper

octopus

CONTENTS

First published 1977 by
Octopus Books Limited
59 Grosvenor Street
London W1

© 1977 Octopus Books Limited

ISBN 0-7064-0666 4

Printed in England by
Severn Valley Press Limited

THE STEWART STORY

Early Days

Rod Stewart's affection for Scotland is a well-known fact. His keen interest in the Scottish football team, Celtic, has become legendary. He was, however, born in Archway Road, North London, the youngest son of Bob and Elsie Stewart. The Stewarts owned a small business which sold newspapers, tobacco and confectionery. Roderick David Stewart was born during the last year of World War II, on January 10, 1945. Plagued with 'flying bombs', at that time London was a hazardous place to live in. Thirty minutes after Rod was born, the police station, only yards from the Stewarts' home, was badly hit by a German V2 rocket.

Rod has always been shy of talking about his childhood but recently told the British newspaper, *The Daily Mirror* 'One of my earliest memories is of the pictures my brothers had on their bedroom walls, they were of Scottish footballers'. Parties were frequent in the Stewart household and many evenings were spent in singing round the piano. Don Stewart used to do skilful impersonations of Al Jolson, the family's favourite musical performer. Although Rod does not regard his family as being particularly musical, their enthusiasm for music doubtless influenced him during his younger days.

Jolson died when Rod was very young but he remembers seeing the films, **The Jazz Singer**, **The Jolson Story** starring Larry Parks, and the follow-up, **Jolson Sings Again**.

Rod remembers how he, as a teenager, set about collecting a complete library of Jolson discs which he still owns. He liked Jolson's performing style and was

Centre: A sharply dressed 'Rod The Mod' (left) seen in 1965 as part of the Steampacket line-up, with John Baldry, Julie Driscoll and Brian Auger.
Left: Members of the Jeff Beck Group with Rod (centre). **Above:** The Downliners, one of the many emergent R & B groups of the early 1960s.

amazed at the way that Al could command an audience of several thousand people without using a microphone or any means of amplification. From his reading of books about Al Jolson, Rod found that they had one thing in common – they both liked playing to a full house.

Rod was a pupil of the William Grimshaw Secondary Modern School in Hornsey. He became a prefect until a few high-spirited escapades upset the school authorities. Football was one of his joys and he captained the school team, showing exceptional skill. He later played in the Schoolboys Team for Middlesex. Three of his school friends were Ray and Dave Davies and Pete Quaife, all later to become part of the successful pop group, the Kinks.

The music of the late 1950s and early 1960s was barely interesting to Rod when he was a teenager. He had a keen awareness of American rock 'n' roll, but the music of artists like Little Richard and Elvis Presley did not interest him. Rod was 18 when the Beatles were having their major successes of 1963, but he was more interested in listening to folk singers than the 'Fab Four'. Folk was fast

developing a social and political identity of its own. Protest songs by such artists as Joan Baez and Bob Dylan captured the imaginations of thousands of young people in Europe and America. In Britain, 'Ban the Bomb' marches were organized by the Campaign for Nuclear Disarmament. Attention was focused on Aldermaston, a centre for nuclear bomb research. Oblivious to the political motives but fired by the atmosphere of the movement, Rod joined the marchers at Easter, 1961 and also marched during the following two years. He once told the British musical paper, *The New Musical Express* that he enjoyed the marches and led the singing as they travelled. He talked of people who marched because it was a place where they could meet the opposite sex.

During the early 1960s Rod enjoyed the music of such 'folkies' as Alex Campbell and The Thames Side Four. He learnt and sang songs by Ramblin' Jack Elliott and Woody Guthrie and particularly admired the work of Derroll Adams. Britain's traditional folk music label, Topic, was a favourite song source and Rod says that he learnt, note by note, songs such as **Cocaine** and **Salty Dog**.

13

He also had a passion for the songs and guitar-playing of Wizz Jones.

Rod's keen interest in football almost persuaded him to become a professional player. He signed forms with Brentford Football Club, a British league club. But his professional career in football was only to last for a few weeks. Bored with the irksome task of cleaning the other players' equipment, Rod soon left the club. His love of football has not left him, however. Rod is a fervent supporter of the Scottish football team, Celtic and an even keener admirer of the Scottish national team. He has, at times, flown 6,000 miles for the opportunity of seeing Scotland play against another nation's team. He will also arrange for a telephone line to link Scotland with whatever country he happens to be in so that he can enjoy a goal-by-goal commentary. He says that he always takes a good supply of footballs with him, wherever he goes, in case there is time for a kick-a-round. He often plays for British show-business football teams in charity matches.

Although Rod listened to folk music and had ideas of becoming a football player, no career really attracted him. He had a series of casual jobs which included working as a gravedigger. He also spent some time hitch-hiking round Europe. In London, he joined the club scene and saw something of the rhythm 'n' blues happenings at the popular Eel Pie Island. His early love for folk music developed into an enthusiasm for R & B music. London and the surrounding area was an exciting and stimulating place. The clubs produced a host of young groups including the Rolling Stones, Who, Birds (including Ron Wood), Yardbirds and Downliners. Rod was there, listening and being influenced by this fascinating music. Even in those days, back in the early 1960s, Wizz Jones thought that Rod was a

During the early 1960s, Rod (below with 'Mod' haircut) listened to the music of such groups as The Who and The Rolling Stones who were playing in the London clubs.

A rare picture of a bearded Stewart with members of the Jeff Beck Group. Bass player Ron Wood (left) was later to join the Faces with Rod.

'pretty flash guy' and had a definite sense of who he was and where he was going.

Rod spent much time learning to play the harmonica and began to look for opportunities to join a band. In 1963 he found himself on stage alongside The Five Dimensions at Ken Colyer's Club in London. He played harmonica for a couple of numbers each evening. The rest of the session was spent watching others, even taking hints from harmonica players such as Mick Jagger. 'I couldn't play the harp at all' Rod told *Zig Zag* magazine 'I used to blow it and wondered why I kept running out of breath.'

For Rod, the opportunity to play two numbers a night was an important start. His career as a musical artist had begun. Rod's early days with The Five Dimensions were fraught with problems and frustrations. It was the legendary meet-ing with Long John Baldry on Twicken-ham railway station which led the way to recognition and professional status for Rod. Baldry invited him to join his band, The Hoochie Coochie Men, as second singer. This band was a continuation of the Rhythm and Blues All Stars, origin-ally led by harmonica-player and singer, Cyril Davies.

In 1964 Rod was 19 and the Beatles were topping the charts with **I Want To Hold Your Hand**. Other Mersey-side artists were producing chart hits, such groups as Freddie and The Dreamers and Gerry and The Pacemakers. The blues music of The Hoochie Coochie Men was not the kind of sound which was hitting the charts at that time but it had a strong following in the R & B clubs. Rod had received a fairly cool reception from the other members of the band but, as his musical ability became apparent he was accepted as a fellow musician and began to develop his stage personality. It was not easy for him at first as he was shy and had never sung blues to a live audience before. John Baldry was a keen follower of authentic American R & B and Rod began to listen to the music of Big Bill Broonzy and Joe Williams. As a band member, Rod gradually became an attraction in his own right as his own indi-vidual style emerged. His nervous habit of ignoring the audience when singing, seemed to impress observers who thought him very cool. The sharply-dressed 'Rod the Mod' created an image which gave him a strong following. Rod, commenting on this period, has said 'I used to be more worried about what I looked like than the music'.

John Baldry usually sang the slower vocals while Rod took the more up-tempo songs. On the B-side of Baldry's **You'll Be Mine**, Rod sang a duet **Up Above My Head** but was not credited on the record label. In October, 1964 Rod's first single was issued by Decca, **Good Morning Little Schoolgirl** backed with **I'm Gonna Move To The Outskirts Of Town**. Session musicians had been booked for the recording and Rod's manager had chosen some com-mercial material for him to record. Rod, however, arrived late for the session and insisted on recording the two blues num-bers which he had heard on a Sonny Boy Williamson album. **Good Morn-ing Little Schoolgirl** was also record-ed by The Yardbirds, but neither version proved to be a chart success. But it did achieve for Rod an appear-ance on Britain's highly-rated TV show **Ready, Steady Go!**

John Baldry decided to turn to a solo career and he disbanded The Hoochie Coochie Men. Rod appeared with the Soul Agents for a few gigs until he re-joined Baldry in a band called Steam-packet. This was a project created by the talented Giorgio Gomelsky, manager of The Yardbirds and several other R & B groups. Steampacket consisted of John Baldry, Rod Stewart, girl vocalist Julie Driscoll, Brian Auger, Rick Brown, Micky Waller and Vic Briggs. The band made no British recordings, although in 1965, some of their material was issued by the French BYG label. During his stay with Steampacket, Rod recorded two singles for Columbia, **The Day Will Come** and **Shake**. **Shake** was written by Sam Cooke who was an artist much admired by Rod at this time. He later said that he owned every single and album ever produced by Cooke. Stew-art regards him as one of his greatest influences and has named **Chain Gang** as the first of the American artist's songs that he ever heard.

Off stage, Steampacket had noisy days with managerial and group arguments. Rod decided to leave and joined up with a band called Shotgun Express. Beryl Marsden was the band's girl vocalist and other members included Peter Green (guitar), Dave Ambrose (bass), Mick Fleetwood (drums), and Peter Bardens (keyboards). Unfortunately the com-bined talents which formed Shotgun

Express never achieved the success which they deserved. Rod recorded one single with the group for Columbia **I Could Feel The Whole World Turn Round** but it did not gain the charts and the group eventually split up. Rod, however, was then set to embark on the most important stage of his early career. This was his association with the guitar-player, Jeff Beck.

Jeff Beck played with The Yardbirds until the end of 1966 and had established a reputation as an accomplished guitarist. At that point he decided to form his own band and tried to bring together such artists as Viv Prince (drummer with The Pretty Things), Jet Harris (previously bass player with The Shadows and then with Tony Meehan), Ron Wood, Rod Stewart and himself. Harris and Prince, however, did not join up with the group. After much swapping and changing the band took to the road for the first time with the line-up of: Stewart (vocals), Beck (guitar), Wood (bass) and Ray Cook (drummer). The group's ill-fated opening night was at London's Astoria, Finsbury Park with The Small Faces topping the bill. Suspected sabotage of the Jeff Beck Group's electrical equipment reduced their volume to a whisper and Jeff Beck angrily walked off the stage. The second house was equally unsuccessful and the band left the tour. Ray Cook left the band and was replaced by Micky Waller.

By May 1967, in spite of their earlier problems, the group had entered the Top Twenty of the British charts with **Hi Ho Silver Lining** backed with **Beck's Bolero**. Jeff Beck sang the vocals on the recording and this disc, although totally unrepresentative of the music style of the group, became a classic British popular record which still continues to sell. The record charted for five weeks, initially. When re-issued in Britain on the RAK label in 1972, it was listed among the Top Twenty singles for four weeks. The band's next single was the instrumental version of **Love Is Blue** with Rod on the B-side singing **I've Been Drinking**, issued in 1968.

In May 1968, The Jeff Beck Group began their first tour of the U.S.A. 'Before the tour we were just treading water in England' said Beck 'just about keeping afloat'. In America the group were caught up in the enthusiasm for British blues which had been started by Cream. Beck had been to America on a number of occasions and had a similar musical background to that of superstar, Eric Clapton. Beck had replaced Clapton when he left The Yardbirds. This band has been termed 'one of the most innovative, second generation bands' by the *New Musical Express History of Rock*. The best of their work is recorded on **The Yardbirds**, issued by Columbia in 1966. The tour of 1968 was a huge success for The Jeff Beck Group, and saw Rod on the road to stardom. They followed up the eight-week tour with an equally successful album, **Truth**. Along with other members of the band, Rod received little credit for his work on the album even though he wrote three songs for the disc. Soon after the release of the album, however, Rod signed a contract with Lou Reizner of Mercury Records, for solo recordings.

In January 1969, The Jeff Beck Group were back in America. Even if British fans had read in their pop papers of the success of The Jeff Beck Group in the U.S.A., they were not given the opportunity to see the group in Britain again. By 1969 Rod had joined The Small Faces.

A further Jeff Beck Group album was issued in the early summer titled **Cosa Nostra Beck-Ola**. This was actually credited 'The Jeff Beck Group' rather than, as with the **Truth** album, merely Jeff Beck. Nicky Hopkins was now a member of the band and Tony Newman had replaced Mickey Waller. The album portrayed a different band, gone was the 'blues' feel, instead it was replaced by a 'heavy metal' sound. Rod and Ron Wood wrote much of what Stewart has called 'silly' lyrics and there was a rough and ready treatment of some rock standards like **All Shook Up** and **Jailhouse Rock**. A single **Plynth (Water Down The Drain)** was taken from the album but it made little impression on the British charts. The band had spent too much time in America, other musical events had come and gone and their established fans had transferred their allegiance elsewhere. During the summer of 1969 rumours circulated that Ron Wood had been practicing with The Small Faces. Beck was evolving plans of forming a new band which would include himself, Stewart, Tim Bogart of the American group, Vanilla Fudge and drummer, Carmine Appice (later to become part of Rod Stewart's own band). His idea never worked out and Ron Wood and Rod Stewart eventually joined The Small Faces.

Rod, looking at his 1967–1969 musical experiences with the Beck Band, was critical of this period, in spite of its importance to his general career development. He said neither he or Jeff had much idea of what they really wanted. They stayed together during this time simply to play together. Along the way they suddenly found themselves with success in America.

Yet in spite of this criticism, Stewart thought that the band was a good one and, in a sense, it never actually broke up, but merely drifted apart. Rod thought that Beck's idea of forming a band with himself, Rod, Tim and Carmine would have had good results. It failed to come together simply because Beck wanted to rehearse in Britain while the others wanted to go to the States.

The original Small Faces line-up, from left to right: Ronnie Lane, Steve Marriott, Kenny Jones and Ian McLagan.

WITH THE FACES

Just Another Face

During the early part of 1969 all kinds of stories had circulated about The Small Faces. Up to this time, the group had accumulated ten British hits including a number three in **Sha La La La Lee**; a chart topper in **All Or Nothing**; a number four with **My Mind's Eye**; number three for the highly regarded, **Itchycoo Park** and during spring of 1968, a position of four in the charts for **Lazy Sunday**. The band had a large following and their line-up comprised Kenny Jones (drums), Steve Marriott (vocals), Ronnie Lane (bass) and Ian McLagan (keyboards). Their fans were suddenly disturbed to read articles in the musical press which talked of the group recording without Marriott. This news was followed by Steve's statement that The Small Faces were soon to split up. In May Ronnie Lane announced to the press that they were looking for someone to replace Marriott.

Ron Wood was one of the influences which caused Rod to join The Small Faces. When Beck broke up the band, Ron had ideas of getting together with Mickey Waller, also sacked from Beck's group, and ex-Blue Cheer guitarist, Leigh Stephens. Wood wished to return to his previous style of guitar-playing and he suggested that Ronnie Lane

should jam with them. The outcome was that Lane was impressed by Ron and suggested that he should see how things worked out with Ian McLagan and Kenny Jones who were the other remaining Small Faces. So Ron joined the band. Rod was a good friend of 'Woody' and used to go along to sessions to listen. The others realised, after a time, that they needed a strong lead voice. Ronnie Lane was not the right person and the trio of Ron Wood, Lane and Ian McLagan did not provide the right vocals together. When Stewart did eventually try out his voice with the band, it proved to be a very promising combination. After playing a few gigs with Art Wood (Ron's brother), John Baldry and Jimmy Horowitz as Quiet Melon, Rod joined The Small Faces. McLagan suggested that the new line-up should have a completely new name. Eventually the band decided to shorten their original name to The Faces.

The musical press informed the fans of Rod's appointment as lead singer during the third week of October 1969. Mercury Records gave Rod permission to record with The Faces and to continue to make solo albums. The Faces (to be) were signed to Warner Brothers for an advance of £30,000. At the beginning of 1970 the band played several gigs as The Small Faces. They

changed their name in the same month as Rod's first solo album **An Old Raincoat Won't Ever Let You Down**, produced by Lou Reizner, was released. This event was celebrated with the release of the single, **Flying**, a joint composition by Wood, Lane and Stewart. The B-side was written by Rod and Ian McLagan and titled, **Three Button Hand Me Down**.

The album, **First Step**, was issued, and it showed that, at this stage, The Faces were very much a group, though not a particularly polished outfit. The major creative force lay in the writing of Ron Wood and Ronnie Lane. Together or solo they were responsible for seven of the nine tracks. Group members, worried about the possibility of Rod Stewart becoming the dominant personality in the group, were not to know that by the third album, their songs would mainly be written by a Wood–Stewart partnership. The Faces toured America during the spring of 1970 and by the autumn, Rod had released his excellent second solo album, **Gasoline Alley**. Now that he was part of The Faces band, it seemed logical that he would use The Faces as backing musicians for his solo discs. Much of Rod's material, however, was very different from that of The Faces. The American tour, with Rod and Ron already having a

reputation dating from the Jeff Beck Group era, was an amazing success and contrasted so vividly with the reaction from British audiences.

During the early days, Rod liked the image which The Faces acquired. It was similar to that of such groups as The Kinks. A reputation for beer, football, cockney humour, and parties appeared very British and gained a strong cult following for The Faces. Their image did not command a broad audience, however, as the prevailing feeling was that musicians must look serious and introspective. The Faces used their ideas of fun both on stage and also off-stage. Endless stories of their high spirits drifted through the bars populated by people in the music business. Reporters swapped stories about the latest hotel prank played by The Faces. It was always hard to decide where truth lay. They were people who enjoyed constant jokes and activities of some kind.

By November 1970, The Faces were in America once more and during the following month they did have some British dates before touring in other European countries. America was visited again in February 1971 for the third time. Stewart flew home during a break in their schedule to work on an album with Long John Baldry and Elton John.

Stewart enjoyed this project and even said that he had surprised himself at what he could do. Stewart felt that the album could really establish Baldry but this did not happen. In March, The Faces' second album was issued, **Long Player**. In June, events for Stewart and The Faces took a dramatic upward turn with the release of Rod's outstanding solo album **Every Picture Tells A Story**. When the single **Maggie May** was released from the album it quickly shot to number one position in the singles and album charts on both sides of the Atlantic.

A month before the Stewart explosion, the British pop paper *The New Musical Express*, via its writer Nick Logan, produced an article, with the headline, 'Why The Faces Are Pleased They Don't Sell Here'. McLagan confirmed that the band were not depressed with Britain, they merely saw it as a long-term objective. He talked to Logan about the bands' 'boozy' reputation and at one point said, 'You get in somewhere in the States and someone you've met there before phones you up: "Heard you were in town, great. Which room you in? Let's wreck a room". But we end up paying the bill.' Ian also said he was a little weary of the material the band had been playing, it had not changed for nearly a year. However, they were working on fresh material and it would come from their **Long Player** album.

The scene changed dramatically within weeks, because of Rod Stewart's success. Rod did not play solo gigs, so if people wanted to see him, they went to The Faces' concerts. The Faces were to

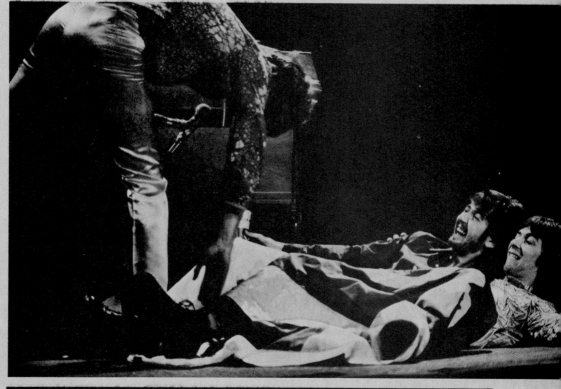

You Can Make Me Dance, Sing Or Anything. The Faces rapidly developed a very lively and extrovert stage presence. They leapt around and produced a spectacle during their stage performances. In those days this behaviour contrasted very sharply with the serious performances of contemporary groups.

Left: Had Me A Real Good Time sums up the band's reputation for drinking and enjoying reckless fun and games. **Above:** Rod looks concerned as a fainting fan is lifted from the stage by members of the road crew. **Below: Debris:** The Faces had a habit of suddenly falling in a heap on the stage.

21

prove themselves with considerable force with their pre-Christmas album **A Nod's As Good As A Wink To A Blind Horse**.

Rod told everyone in July, and early-August, that the success of his album was, for him, the culmination of six years of hard work. He had, according to Bill McAllister of Britain's *Record Mirror*, become a singer's singer and now he was the people's singer. Stewart recalled, in an interview, how his first two albums meant little in Britain and he thought 'it was all down to America and maybe Europe' but now, with the success of **Maggie May** and **Every Picture Tells A Story**, it was developing as he had hoped.

Inevitably, his stunning solo success, with much attention directed at him personally, meant that people would begin asking whether he would merely continue to front the group. Rod, for much of the time, was content to say that he was just a member of The Faces. Stewart said that the release of albums would have to be carefully planned for it seemed pointless to have himself and The Faces competing against one another. He thought that his next recording would be with The Faces, giving a late 1971 album release. It would also mean he wouldn't have much time left for solo recording. He expressed determination to do all that he could to ensure success for the next Faces' album. Stewart had also noticed that American fans were beginning to copy his haircut and style of dress. Barbers even asked him how he got his individual effect! Stewart's answer to this question was that it had taken six years of torture to get it the way that he wanted it. When Rod was asked if he would play solo concerts, he said that everything has its season and it might just happen, if the other band members agreed to back him on stage. He thought it much more likely that he would include his own solo numbers on stage as part of a Faces' concert.

Whilst Rod's album was the talking point, The Faces were touring America once more and Rod met Dee Harrington, who was to become his steady girl-friend, at a Los Angeles party. In September 1971, the group won British acclaim by playing some brilliant sets at The Weeley Festival followed by a special charity concert for Bangladesh, at London's Oval Cricket Ground, where the band appeared with The Who.

The fifth Faces' tour took place in November of 1971. The band were confident in the knowledge that their latest album, **Long Player**, which featured Wood–Stewart compositions, had been greeted with enthusiastic response. When they played at Madison Square Garden, New York, a stadium which seated 20,000 people, tickets were sold out several weeks before the concert.

There was a British date in February 1972, but American tours became by far the most important part of their pro-

gramme. During April, they took part in a Rock 'n' Roll Circus with Fleetwood Mac. There were clowns, jugglers, acrobats, and a Chinese lady performing a striptease fifty feet above the audience. Memphis, Tennessee saw the circus first, with the band playing beneath a huge beige and green dome. This possibly gave Ronnie Lane the idea for his solo venture several years later, though his marquee was very much smaller. On this occasion, in Memphis, The Faces were hit by travelling problems. Their two hour flight took over five hours but they arrived in time to cool the crowd which was beginning to get restless. Rod, who was now a very popular subject for the American fashion magazines, wore blue sneakers, a yellow and black mock tiger suit with a yellow silk scarf. Lane, in contrast, wore a 1950s 'Teddy Boy' drape suit, coloured blue, with white cuffs, pockets and collar. The band had difficulty getting organized. They hadn't played for about six weeks and they were a little rusty and slightly lacking in musical cohesion. Tired as they were, however, the Faces still managed to achieve their now famous mixture of good music and colourful stage behaviour. They leapt and danced their way through numbers like **That's All You Need** and **Gasoline Alley**. After the concert, Stewart spoke of his pleasure at seeing the band now making an impact in Britain. He recalled how The Faces had been regarded on many occasions as just a backing band. Now people were flocking to see them. Rod said that he found the pop scene a 'funny old business'.

Britain heard the band in May. They were part of the massive Great Western Festival at Bardney, Lincolnshire. The list of groups seemed like a *Who's Who* of British talent of that time. There were a few American acts on the billing but the majority of bands were British. Several months later, Rod's fourth solo album was issued, **Never A Dull Moment**. Stewart featured Dylan songs again and spoke of his respect for the American singer-songwriter. He also drew the reviewer's attention to the sleeve-notes

A look at the serious side of the Faces as they rehearse before a major concert in the USA. **Right:** After rehearsing the band enjoy a drink in their dressing room.

22

where there was a plea that the album should be considered for itself alone and opinion should not be influenced by the previous massive seller, **Every Picture Tells A Story**. Stewart expressed, during conversation, his fear that in the future no one would allow him the luxury of a bad or imperfect track. Yet, in spite of these fears, Stewart, in his self-confident way, proclaimed **Never A Dull Moment** as being better than the last album and that he had a personal liking for every track on the disc. In **Every Picture Tells A Story**, he had been a little disappointed with **Seems Like A Long Time**, **That's Alright Mama** and **Amazing Grace**, though at the same time, he thought that nothing on the new album could compare with **Mandolin Wind** his favourite track. Rod also expressed a desire to make an album of singles, rather in the K-Tel hit album image.

Stewart, talking to Nick Logan, of *New Musical Express* for August 8, 1972, took exception to the paper's comment that The Faces should come up with an album as good as **Every Picture Tells A Story**. Stewart said, 'I don't think there ever will be that day because my and the group's albums are so completely different'. He pointed out that there were differences even in the backing provided by The Faces. He pointed out Ron Wood's increased lead-playing on the solo albums. Also when he, Rod, sang with The Faces, he tended to indulge in screaming and shouting sessions. Stewart defended albums from The Faces and argued that their **Nod's As Good As A Wink To A Blind Horse** was on a par with the Rolling Stones disc, **Sticky Fingers**. He did, however, believe that his albums had a broader appeal for a listening and record buying public, though in stage performances, it was the other way round for, there, people preferred cuts off the **Nod** album.

Logan also talked to Rod about the growing cult of glam-rock, with such artists as Bolan and Bowie, wearing exotic clothes, make-up and arresting hair styles. Stewart seemed amused by the efforts of some people to claim that they were the first to adopt this kind of style. He thought that their use of glam-rock gear and cosmetics was only temporary.

Whilst Stewart enjoyed the success of **Never A Dull Moment**, plans were being made to release a track under the title of Python Lee Jackson, with Stewart singing vocal for a song, **In A Broken Dream**. On the Youngblood label, it charted in the Top 20 and reached the top ten, spending over two months in the top listing. The story behind the recording came in an October issue of *Record Mirror*, in 1972. There, it was said, DJ and then co-Dandelion record owner, John Peel had signed a group from Australia, Python Lee Jackson to his label. The group had a

talented writer, David Bentley, and a fine guitarist, but they were not successful in the studio. A few tracks, one of which was **In A Broken Dream**, had been recorded. Rod Stewart was asked if he would put down the vocal track. This he did. Peel did not want to release a record with a session singer taking the major lead on the disc and he sold the tapes to Youngblood. They were re-mixed, some additional mellotron was added and a hit was born for Python Lee Jackson.

In November, of 1972, **Angel** was issued as a single, from **Never A Dull Moment**. In December, Rod appeared in the London stage production of the rock opera, **Tommy**, written by Pete Townshend of The Who. Rod played the 'local lad' and sang **Pinball Wizard**. During the Christmas month, The Faces toured Britain. 1972 had been a good year for Rod. The Faces had achieved acceptance by British audiences and they had produced a good album. They had also had a successful series of tours in the U.S.A.

Rod had grown confident. He had become quite the opposite to the artist who, on the early Jeff Beck tours of America, had kept out of the way because he was nervous. He now said that he could start a riot at any concert if he wished. He thought that The Faces' songs and very presence could make an audience leave their seats and come crowding to the front of the stage. Stewart said that his act was well controlled and if anyone wished to compare his performances with another artist then, it would be with someone like Mick Jagger. Rod expressed a feeling that he might find himself too over-exposed as an artist and he was bothered by an apparent lack of time. He was determined, somehow during 1973, to resolve his problem of how to devote enough time to Faces' recordings and to his own. This was something which he was never to solve until he finally made the break and formed his own band four years later.

He spoke of his future as someone who would have an established audience.

He didn't forsee himself becoming involved with production as he found it boring. For him, as an artist, he needed people and nothing exhilarated him more than seeing faces 'out there'. If he had more courage, Rod said, he would love to try becoming an actor. During this period Rod also spoke to the press of his attitude towards money; how he relaxed, and his personal fears. Without hesitating he said that money was important to him, and (at that time) his earnings were invested in Jersey. As to what monies he possessed, that was a private affair, he would merely say that he was doing fine! For relaxation, he chose football. He found music a tiring business and usually felt pretty worn out after a session at writing lyrics. Football provided a good way of unwinding followed by, of course, a good pint of beer. He also enjoyed cooking and hunting for antique furniture and often took days off to relax down in Cornwall. As for the 'fear' in his life, this was a flying phobia. He thought that he must be second only to the musician, Alan Price, in his fear of flying. He wished that 'planes would follow the freeways from a height of just a hundred feet!

Kenny Jones spoke to the press at the

beginning of 1973 and he told of times during 1972 when the band had been very bored. He said they had vowed that they would average around three gigs a week, in 1973. He, himself, was busy taking part in a recording session with Jerry Lee Lewis, whilst the American artist was in London. He said that they would like to try out other ideas such as film-making. There was always the dual problem, however, of trying to run a band and, at the same time, making allowances for the continuation of Rod's solo career. Kenny also spoke about press criticism when The Faces cancelled some dates to enable him to be with his wife when their baby was born during 1972. To him, this criticism was part of the strange nature of the musical press which was capable of making

1972, they had sounded slightly rusty but no more than that. They were soon playing smoothly together. He had few words on the subject of Rod and his relationship with the band. He merely said that it had ceased to be a real problem. The difficulties were accepted and the band just carried on, as best as the varying conditions allowed. He did agree that the band was a mixed bunch of people but, even if they looned around, there was remarkable cohesion when circumstances demanded it.

In February of 1973, a Faces single **Cindy Incidentally** was issued, with Rod credited as one of the three writers of the song. One of Britain's pop music papers, *Disc*, voted Rod as the top British and World singer. At times Rod made rather disparaging remarks about

members would retire to a bar and, often only after closing time, did they begin recording. Still, whether the album was good or not, The Faces themselves were playing well. Rod insisted that, even if he was uncomplimentary about the disc, it did not mean that he was considering a split from the group and he regarded the band as a life partnership. He spoke of the impending visit to America and also of his own future album on which he hoped he could include some songs from the Sutherland Brothers.

When The Faces returned from their U.S.A. tour of 1973, the first serious split in the band occurred. Ronnie Lane announced that 'It was time for him to move on'. This was hardly surprising, for Rod had become very influential in both writing material and singing it. Ronnie's more homely music was becoming less and less relevant to the kind of musical style and act being presented by the band. Lane was also upset by the amount of publicity which Rod was receiving. The press had also criticised some of his songs which had appeared on Faces' albums.

So, The Faces found themselves with a vacancy. They approached Andy Fraser, who had just left Sharks but he declined. They auditioned for a bass player and eventually they chose Tetsu Yamauchi, a Japanese musician who had been Andy Fraser's substitute when the latter had left Free. His membership of the band was complicated by problems with the Musicians' Union over his right to work in Britain. However, once these problems were resolved he proved to be an excellent asset to the band and helped the others to achieve a tighter sound.

In July, British record company, Mercury, issued a compilation album called **Sing It Again, Rod**, consisting of tracks from Mercury and Vertigo albums. It earned Stewart another Gold Disc. The European tour which was cancelled in June was re-scheduled for July and it was the first series of performances featuring Tetsu Yamauchi. During August, The Faces played several British gigs and the same month saw the release of a Goffin and King number, **Oh No, Not My Baby**, as Rod's next single. He called it his first bona fide single since **You Wear It Well**, as **Angel** had been released without his consent. He also surprised some people by telling the press that he would make only one more solo album. He had visions of calling it 'Scotland For The Royal Cup'. Rod's explanation for this threat was lack of time. Rod, in the summer of 1973, thought that he was now at the crossroads of his career. He told Chris Welch of Britain's, *Melody Maker*, that he still enjoyed being an idol, that his voice was as good as ever and his current ambition was to make a really good Rod Stewart LP. **'Nod's As Good As A Wink'** was the

complimentary approving noises and then, when it suited them, they would take the opposite stand. He challenged the assertions that the Faces didn't worry about what they were doing. He argued that the band was performing a great number of gigs and that they attempted to give their fans value for money by paying extra attention to their own printed programmes; and at Christmas time they always tried to put more effort into their stage decor and their performances. He also attacked those who said that the band was always playing the same numbers and remarked that, surely people wished to hear the old favourites. There was also some criticism of the band's playing which he wished to answer. He agreed that, at the beginning of their December tour of

Left: A typical Faces pose, which enhanced their boozy reputation. **Above:** Drinking again! The Faces meet photographers in the foyer of a Manchester hotel. Standing on the right is Tetsu Yamauchi, the Japanese bass player.

awards, but he changed his mind, particularly when he realised that the awards reflected the affection of the fans.

In the Spring of 1973, The Faces' album **Ooh La La** was issued. Rod responded by stating quite firmly that he found the disc a 'mess'. Stewart said that the reason for the current Faces' recording 'mess' lay in their whole approach to making a disc. It was always a problem for The Faces to get anything done. Kenny Jones would arrive first but he and other

Rod Stewart gradually began to dominate the line-up and developed a stage personality which attracted and captured the Faces audiences.

best band LP we made and **Gasoline Alley** was my best solo LP so far'.

The autumn of 1973 saw The Faces back in the States for a five week tour and to the *Los Angeles Times*, Ron Wood commented, 'We still like to party at the slightest excuse but we've tried to maintain a bit of sanity in the dressing rooms before and after a show. I think the difference is that we now choose when we want to go mad. We still flip, though'. And, earlier, in the year, The Faces had stunned the pop fraternity by having 2,000 backstage passes printed for the tour, in comparison with a more normal 120 or 125. There had been crazy scenes backstage at the Nassau Colliseum in New York. October of 1973 saw the release of The Faces single, **Pool Hall Richard** coupled with **I Wish It Would Rain**.

The second week of November saw the British pop papers announcing dates for the late November/December tour of The Faces. It would start at The Granada, East Ham on November 29 and reach its finale with a Christmas Eve show at Sundown, Edmonton, London. Two dates were left clear, December 13 and 14, for Rod to take part in a production of **Tommy** at London's Rainbow. Meantime, while people were setting up the British tour, Rod was being photographed running around the pitch of Watford football club with Elton John. It was part of Rod's get-fit campaign for the oncoming tour. At the same time, Rod had been seen with Paul McCartney and Elton John at the Morgan Studios, Willesden, north-

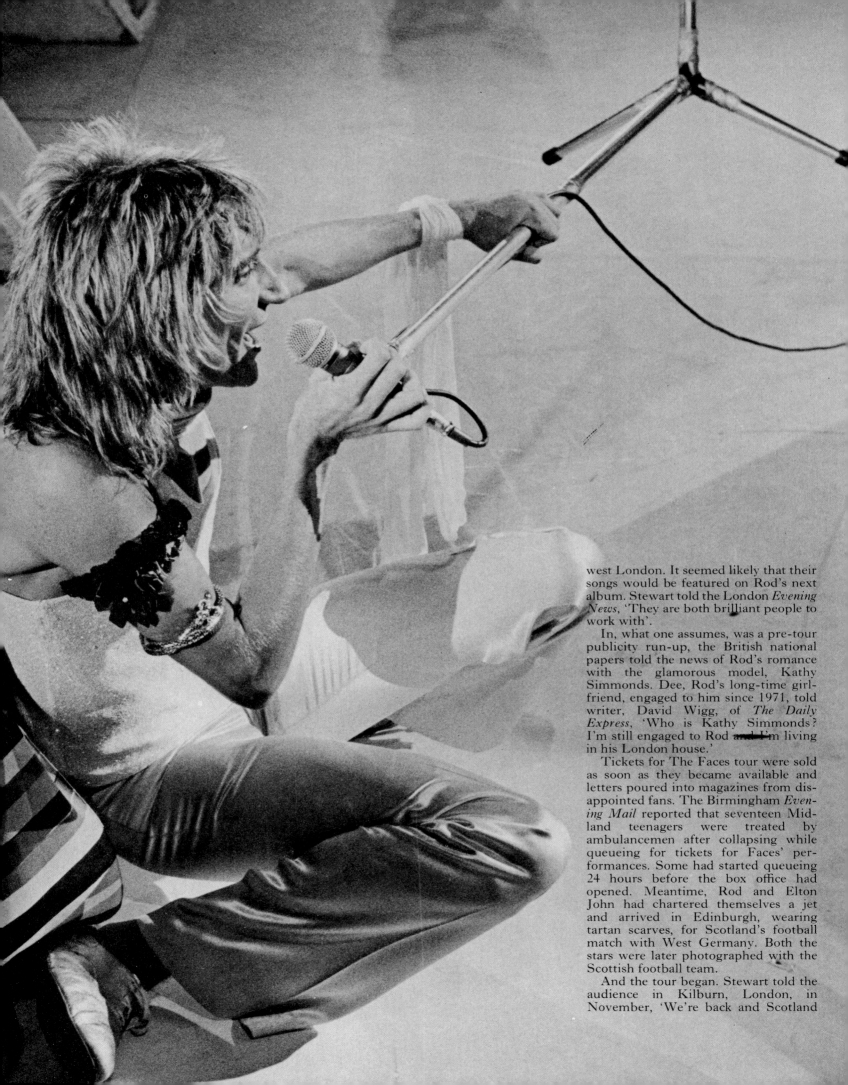

west London. It seemed likely that their songs would be featured on Rod's next album. Stewart told the London *Evening News*, 'They are both brilliant people to work with'.

In, what one assumes, was a pre-tour publicity run-up, the British national papers told the news of Rod's romance with the glamorous model, Kathy Simmonds. Dee, Rod's long-time girl-friend, engaged to him since 1971, told writer, David Wigg, of *The Daily Express*, 'Who is Kathy Simmonds? I'm still engaged to Rod ~~and I'm~~ living in his London house.'

Tickets for The Faces tour were sold as soon as they became available and letters poured into magazines from dis-appointed fans. The Birmingham *Evening Mail* reported that seventeen Midland teenagers were treated by ambulancemen after collapsing while queueing for tickets for Faces' per-formances. Some had started queueing 24 hours before the box office had opened. Meantime, Rod and Elton John had chartered themselves a jet and arrived in Edinburgh, wearing tartan scarves, for Scotland's football match with West Germany. Both the stars were later photographed with the Scottish football team.

And the tour began. Stewart told the audience in Kilburn, London, in November, 'We're back and Scotland

are going to win the World Cup'. This concert was not particularly stimulating, however, and lacked cohesion. Rod sang some good blues material but there was little excitement, except that which was generated by the fans.

At Bristol, on December 2, there was more energy from the band and Rod was truly warming up. The city's *Evening Post*, related that 'The Faces superstar circus rolled into Bristol last night for a boozy; clowning and completely deafening show at the Hippodrome' and commented that in their view, Rod gave a massive send-up of the whole rock-star syndrome. Stewart, said that the paper's writer, James Belsey, had style.

The band opened the year 1974 by touring in Australia and New Zealand. A live album, **Rod Stewart and The Faces** was released and more British gigs followed. A Faces' maxi-single was issued in June and comprised **Cindy Incidentally**, **Memphis**, **Stay With Me** and **Pool Hall Richard**. In July, the band topped the bill at the Buxton Festival. There, Stewart and the band enjoyed one of their most successful performances augmented by the Memphis Horns.

A month or so later, Stewart talked to the music press about his views on tax, The Faces and their fans and his own personal career problems. He looked well, having just returned from Spain

Lifting and twirling his mike stand, Rod makes full use of the stage to create and project his image. **Above and below:** Rod Stewart and Ron Wood duet on stage.

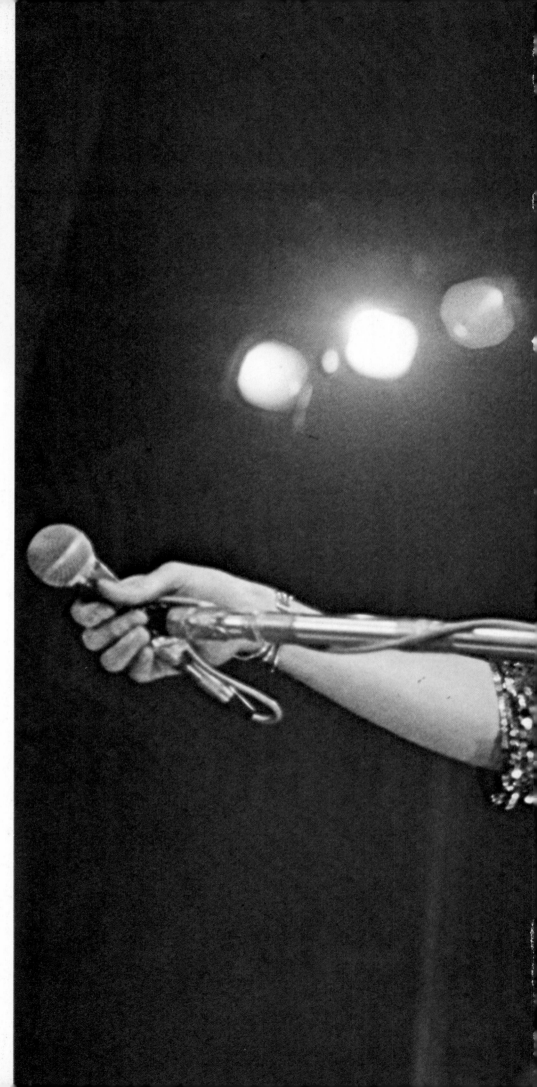

Rod, expressive on stage, gives everything to his audience.

where he had, among other things, taken up golf under the tutorship of Sean Connery. Rod posed for photographers but took exception to interviewers with tape-machines. His humour came across in the interviews together with the kind of flair which instinctively draws from the listener a liking for the artist. Stewart said that he had worked hard all his life and now his earnings were being eaten up by excessive taxation. His own personal problems involved never-ending recording contractual squabbles and Phonogram and Warner Brothers were fighting over the right to record him. Rod spoke of the completed **Smiler** album but there was no release date in view. He was not particularly forthcoming about its content but he admitted that one cut would be **Girl From The North Country**. He merely said that he would not record a cover-version of a song, unless he thought he could do a better version. This was the case with his recording of Sam Cooke's **Twistin' The Night Away** where he felt that he had up-dated this standard. When asked about the future of the band he said that a European tour was planned for the autumn. Stewart also said that he felt that band members were getting much more involved with their indi-vidual projects. He suggested that the group may not make any more albums but only singles.

In August, the group played at three American festivals and in autumn the European tour ended in Britain. While The Faces toured, Ron Wood's solo album, **I've Got My Own Album To Do** was released and on the album credits, appeared the names of Mick Jagger, Mick Taylor and Keith Richard. A single was released by Rod in Sep-tember which had three tracks: **Fare-well**, **Bring It On Home To Me** and

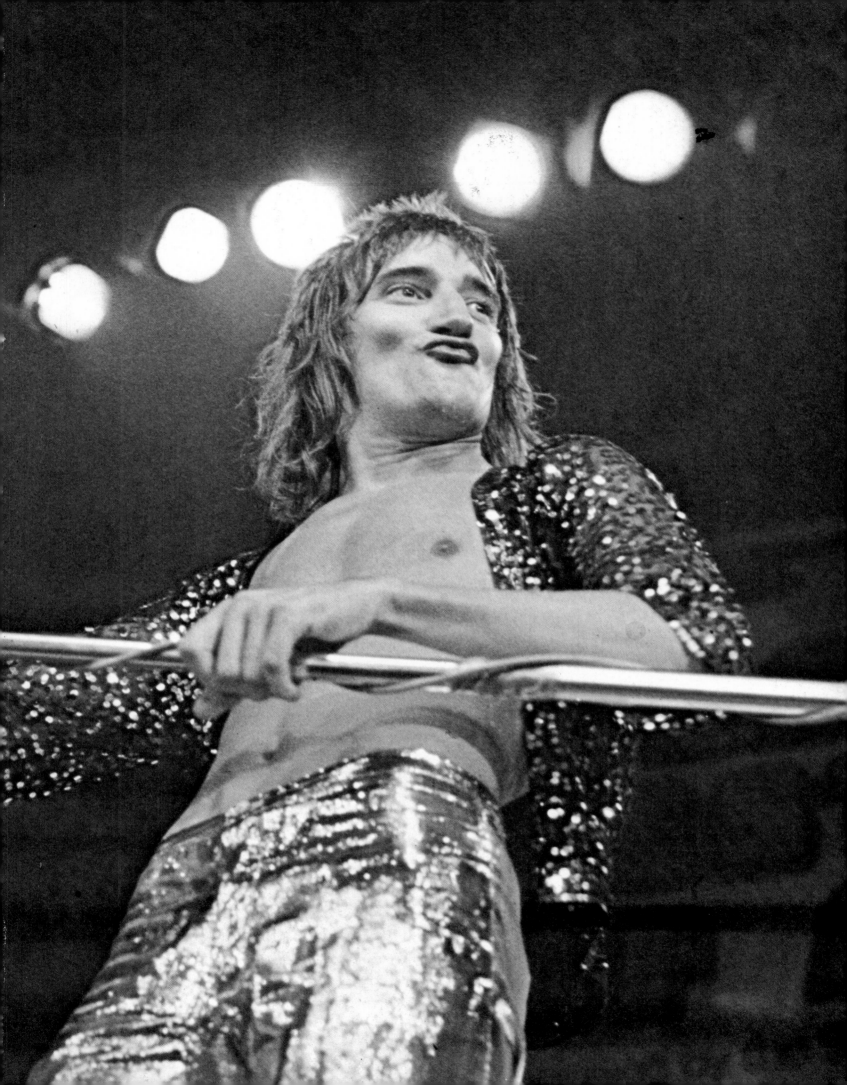

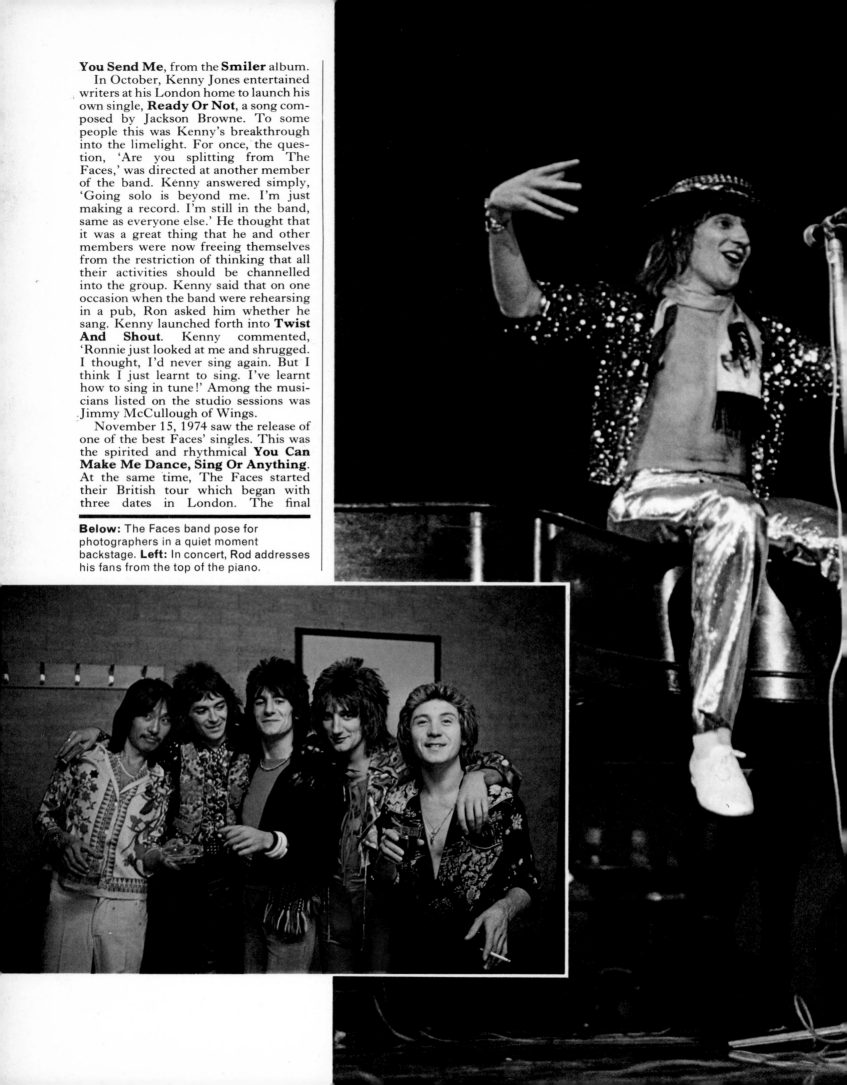

You Send Me, from the **Smiler** album.

In October, Kenny Jones entertained writers at his London home to launch his own single, **Ready Or Not**, a song composed by Jackson Browne. To some people this was Kenny's breakthrough into the limelight. For once, the question, 'Are you splitting from The Faces,' was directed at another member of the band. Kenny answered simply, 'Going solo is beyond me. I'm just making a record. I'm still in the band, same as everyone else.' He thought that it was a great thing that he and other members were now freeing themselves from the restriction of thinking that all their activities should be channelled into the group. Kenny said that on one occasion when the band were rehearsing in a pub, Ron asked him whether he sang. Kenny launched forth into **Twist And Shout**. Kenny commented, 'Ronnie just looked at me and shrugged. I thought, I'd never sing again. But I think I just learnt to sing. I've learnt how to sing in tune!' Among the musicians listed on the studio sessions was Jimmy McCullough of Wings.

November 15, 1974 saw the release of one of the best Faces' singles. This was the spirited and rhythmical **You Can Make Me Dance, Sing Or Anything**. At the same time, The Faces started their British tour which began with three dates in London. The final

Below: The Faces band pose for photographers in a quiet moment backstage. **Left:** In concert, Rod addresses his fans from the top of the piano.

Above: Ian McLagan, talented Faces'
keyboard player and (below) Tetsu
Yamauchi, the bass player whose steady
rhythms held the band's music tightly
together.

British Christmas Concert at the Kilburn Gaumont was filmed and shown on British TV.

Early in 1975, The Faces set off on a two-month tour of the States. The Rolling Stones asked Ron Wood if he would like to take Mick Taylor's place in their line-up but he turned down this offer. Rod told the *New Musical Express* in January that there had been a lot of arguing among The Faces members and feelings had run high at times but at that time, things had never been better.

In the spring, tours of Britain and the States were announced for later in the autumn. This reassured some fans as to the band's stability, but others were worried when it was learnt that Rod had flown to America to record a new album and that there would be no Faces members among his backing musicians. Stewart also announced that he intended to set up permanent residence in the States and would be applying for citizenship. This put the other Faces'

members into the position of having to decide whether they would also leave Britain and settle in America. When Kenny Jones talked to Britain's *Daily Express* in July, more doubts were cast on the band's future. Jones complained that Rod had seriously affected his earnings. He said that he hadn't worked for four months and his income was affected by the cancellation of the projected Faces' summer concerts in Britain. The Faces' managers said that it was all a misunderstanding and Rod would speak to Kenny about it.

August saw Rod, unable for tax reasons to enter Britain, in Ireland with his new love, Britt Ekland. Stewart held a press conference to launch his **Atlantic Crossing** album but, inevitably, he talked about his relationship with The Faces and the recent public statements. He said that he could not really foresee the future with any clarity and thought that Kenny Jones had been unfair in his accusations. Rod said that the band were all going to live in America (apart from Ron Wood the others declined to do so). Rod said that the British summer concerts were never viable as Ron was touring with the Rolling Stones.

Other remarks which Rod made were not popular with some of The Faces. Ian MacLagan said that he was hurt by a remark which suggested that the group was musically sloppy, but Rod had denied he had said it. However, amidst arguments and journalistic gossip, a new Faces tour was confirmed. Other rumours circulated, however. It was said that Kenny and Ian were thinking of re-grouping with Steve Marriott and Ronnie Lane to form a Small Faces reunion tour. They assumed that Rod would pursue a solo career and Ron would perhaps finally decide to join the Rolling Stones.

The single, **Sailing**, from the **Atlantic Crossing** album was issued in August backed with **Stone Cold Sober**. In the same month, The Faces were back on the road for a 35-city tour of the U.S.A. but not without tension. It was not long before the announcement came that Rod would be quitting The Faces. The statement avoided any controversy with The Faces as a group, or Rod's recent recording activities without them, and nor did it mention Rod's own change of circumstances being a British tax-exile. Instead, Tony Toon, head of publicity, said 'Rod feels he can no longer work in a situation where the group's lead guitarist, Ron Wood, seems to be permanently on loan to the Rolling Stones.' And The Faces manager, Billy Gaff, said 'Rod thinks the world of Ron Wood. I have repeatedly tried to telephone Ron, who is touring Europe with the Stones. I have left messages for him to call me, but I've heard nothing.'

According to the *New Musical Express*, Ian MacLagan said that he would not believe the statement unless Rod in-

formed him personally whilst Kenny Jones calmly said he wasn't too put-out.

On reflection, Britain's *Melody Maker*, said in February 1977 'Rod began to feel . . . an increasing realization that he could work better on his own, or at least with musicians where he could call more of the shots.'

Always a showman, Stewart kneels to his audience, festooned with tartan muffler (left) and dramatically lit with sequins (right). It has been said of Rod that he

In some ways, it was remarkable that the Rod Stewart/Faces liaison survived as long as it did. Perhaps this illustrated clearly the personality of Rod Stewart. He seemed someone who greatly enjoyed being one of the boys, and yet, at the same time, felt the pull of a world which could make him a star.

satisfies 'the Scottish need for tartan, the gay world's need for glamour, the rock world's lust for glory and the public's love of foppery'.

STATESIDE
STEWART

Rod Stewart achieved success in America long before Britain became aware of his musical merits and style. In 1968 he went with the Jeff Beck Band across the Atlantic to tour the U.S.A. Beck was already known in the States, for he was associated with some of the young British blues musicians who were beginning to gain an American following.

In the early days Stewart was nervous on stage, hiding himself and ignoring the audience. As he gained confidence he began to adopt an extrovert stage performance which became very popular with his American audiences. *Creem* writer, Mac Garry said that Beck, Rod and the others came on as if they were not performing for money but solely for the people out-front. Mac Garry said, 'most of us were dazed – even the straights . . . devastating . . .' Beck with Rod, and the others, suddenly saw an enormous market awaiting them. Jeff once said of their producer Mickie Most, who had controlled their British releases, that when he saw the band in action in the U.S.A., he exclaimed, 'What have I been doing all this time?'

When he toured the U.S.A. later with The Faces, Rod was again a massive hit with American audiences, long before

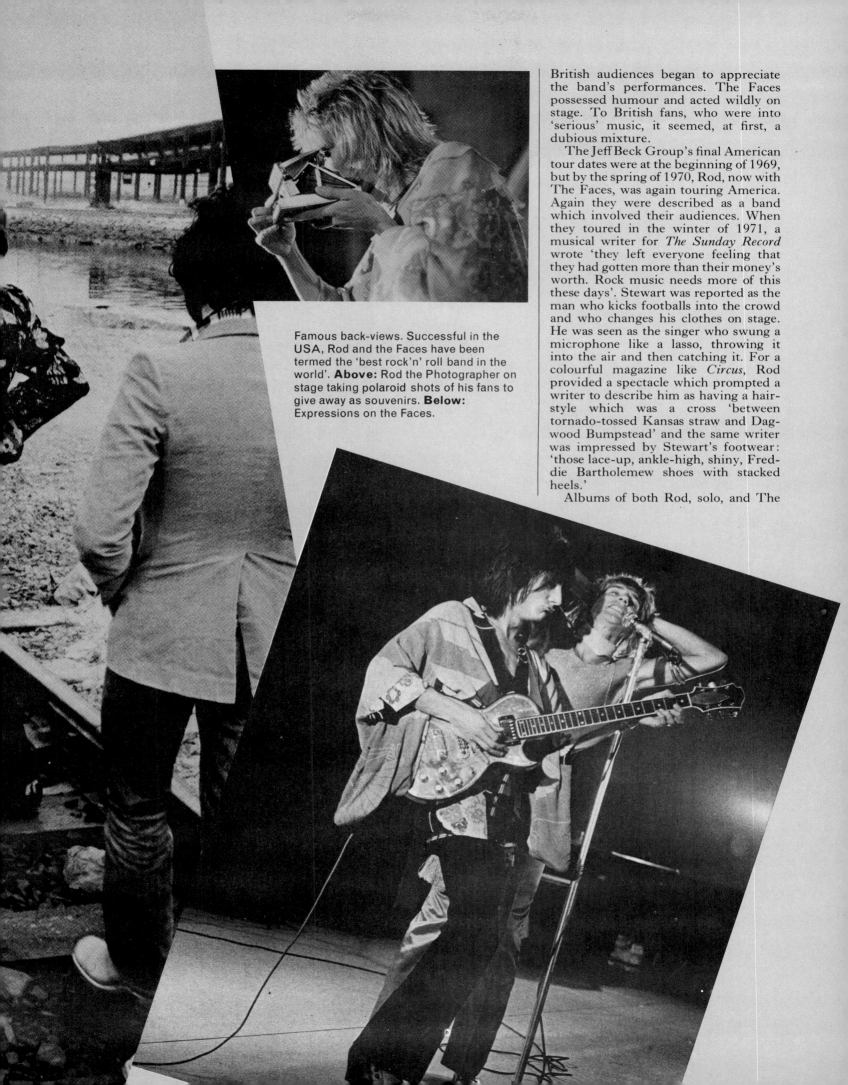

British audiences began to appreciate the band's performances. The Faces possessed humour and acted wildly on stage. To British fans, who were into 'serious' music, it seemed, at first, a dubious mixture.

The Jeff Beck Group's final American tour dates were at the beginning of 1969, but by the spring of 1970, Rod, now with The Faces, was again touring America. Again they were described as a band which involved their audiences. When they toured in the winter of 1971, a musical writer for *The Sunday Record* wrote 'they left everyone feeling that they had gotten more than their money's worth. Rock music needs more of this these days'. Stewart was reported as the man who kicks footballs into the crowd and who changes his clothes on stage. He was seen as the singer who swung a microphone like a lasso, throwing it into the air and then catching it. For a colourful magazine like *Circus*, Rod provided a spectacle which prompted a writer to describe him as having a hair-style which was a cross 'between tornado-tossed Kansas straw and Dagwood Bumpstead' and the same writer was impressed by Stewart's footwear: 'those lace-up, ankle-high, shiny, Freddie Bartholemew shoes with stacked heels.'

Albums of both Rod, solo, and The

Famous back-views. Successful in the USA, Rod and the Faces have been termed the 'best rock'n' roll band in the world'. **Above:** Rod the Photographer on stage taking polaroid shots of his fans to give away as souvenirs. **Below:** Expressions on the Faces.

Faces enjoyed success in the U.S.A. By the time the band toured the States from November 23, 1971 onwards, three of Rod's solo albums were hits, and **Maggie May** had been a chart success. Tickets for The Faces' concerts were sold out instantly.

The strongest indication of The Faces' success in the U.S.A. was when they played to a packed house at New York's Madison Square Garden stadium. For their concert of November 26, 1971, they used two huge closed-circuit colour screens with a large green and white banner stretched between them which read **A Nod's As Good As A Wink To A Blind Horse**, the name of their latest album. The stage setting was large but The Faces were a match for it. Richard Gold, writer for the journal *Rock* talked of Rod being the 'master of primal power' directing a 'boogie-crazed mob'. Gold felt that he and the group win over their audiences by sheer force. Gold travelled West with the band and marvelled at Rod's performances which he described as 'moments of sculptured grace' and 'utterly incredible fits of lunatic frenzy'. On this tour, The Faces took with them a black dancer, Charlie Daniels, known as the 'master blaster' from Boston. The

Far left: A characteristic Woody with hat and drooping cigarette. **Left:** Kenny Jones impassively holds the beat.

Above and below: Tetsu Yamauchi gives the bass and adds his own individual style to the band's performances.

Massive, enthusiastic audiences greeted the Faces on their frequent tours of the USA. At an out-door concert at Santa Barbara, fans go wild for brown-skinned Rod with his sun-streaked mane of hair.

Faces travelled expensively by chartered jet plane and chauffeured limousines, but expenses were no worry to the band as they could expect to receive $30,000 to $50,000 for one performance.

In 1975, Rod and The Faces were on tour in the U.S.A. again to promote **Atlantic Crossing**, Rod's first disc to be entirely recorded in the States. His American fans and the music critics began to wonder at this stage whether Rod would stay with The Faces. 55,000 Stewart and Faces' fans in Los Angeles saw the band play a very ragged set which was due to their equipment and instruments being stranded in a truck on a freeway. Make-shift amplifiers and microphones kept breaking down and the overall sound was muddy. Stewart seemed in good humour as he dashed from one microphone to another and worked tirelessly to involve the audience and make the best of the situation. Near the end of the set even Rod's coolness evaporated and he suddenly picked up a dead microphone and furiously ham-

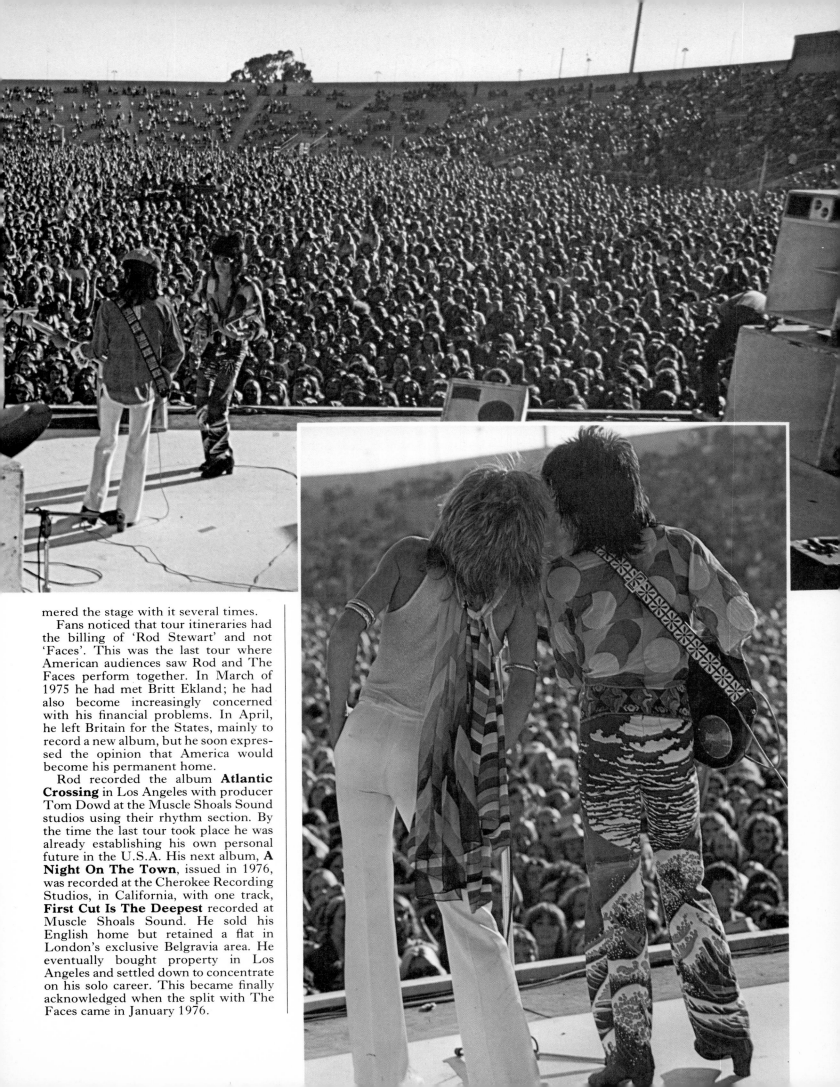

mered the stage with it several times.

Fans noticed that tour itineraries had the billing of 'Rod Stewart' and not 'Faces'. This was the last tour where American audiences saw Rod and The Faces perform together. In March of 1975 he had met Britt Ekland; he had also become increasingly concerned with his financial problems. In April, he left Britain for the States, mainly to record a new album, but he soon expressed the opinion that America would become his permanent home.

Rod recorded the album **Atlantic Crossing** in Los Angeles with producer Tom Dowd at the Muscle Shoals Sound studios using their rhythm section. By the time the last tour took place he was already establishing his own personal future in the U.S.A. His next album, **A Night On The Town**, issued in 1976, was recorded at the Cherokee Recording Studios, in California, with one track, **First Cut Is The Deepest** recorded at Muscle Shoals Sound. He sold his English home but retained a flat in London's exclusive Belgravia area. He eventually bought property in Los Angeles and settled down to concentrate on his solo career. This became finally acknowledged when the split with The Faces came in January 1976.

Above: Rod Stewart and the Faces band travelling and rehearsing during a tour of the USA. **Right:** Glitter-clad and framed in stage lighting, Rod extends his arms in a dramatic appeal to his audience.

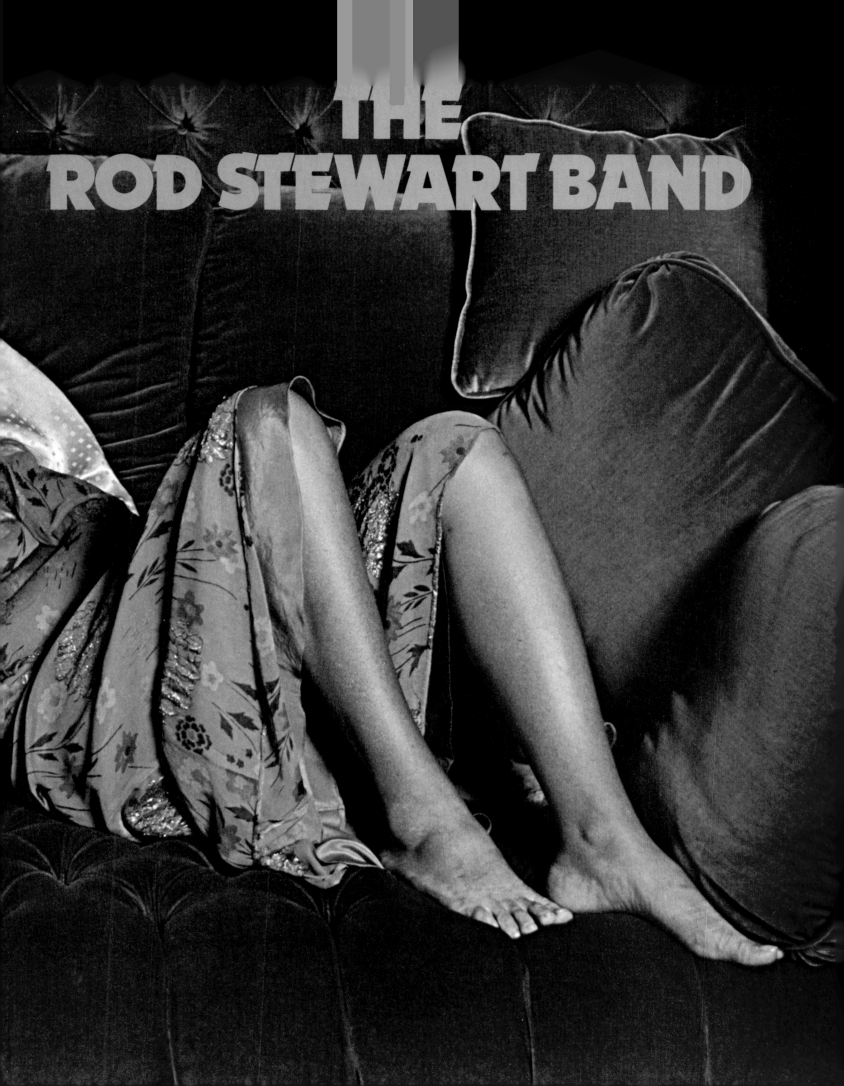

THE
ROD STEWART BAND

Gary Grainger was born in Kilburn, North London. He began his music career as a drummer but was converted to the electric guitar by the music of The Shadows and Buddy Holly. During 1974 Grainger toured with the Faces as a member of Strider. He made a lasting impression on Rod who selected him for his band. Grainger says 'We all have different ways of playing. I'm more the raunchy kind of player'.

Billy Peek has spent most of his musical career playing guitar with Chuck Berry and has been named the rock 'n' roller of the Stewart Band. Born in St Louis, Peek became interested in music by listening to his father's guitar-playing. Stewart spotted Peek on a television programme playing with Chuck Berry, and he played on Rod's **A Night On The Town album**. Peek says of his music 'when it comes to rock 'n' roll, I can play it'.

Jim Cregan, guitarist, was born in Somerset, England. He has played with the jazz-rock band Taste and also Family. His most recent musical associations are with Steve Harley and Cockney Rebel. and jazz singer Linda Lewis (now his wife). Cregan is a sensitive guitarist and complements his fellow-guitarists in the band. He says 'Billy Peek is untouchable in the rock 'n' roll tunes while the rest of the work is between Gary and myself'.

After The Faces

In 1975, much press attention was focused on the growing split between Rod Stewart and the other Faces. Rod was not the only band member to be considering a solo career, but he proved to be the catalyst which finally ended their association. **Atlantic Crossing**, recorded with producer Tom Dowd, was possibly the album which convinced Rod that he had achieved the sound which he had been moving towards. He was now ready to work without The Faces and establish his own identity.

When Rod arrived in London to promote **A Night On The Town**, in the summer of 1976, it was thought that Rod was then looking around for the kind of artists who he wanted for his projected first solo tour, which, like the recent Wings tour, would include most of the countries in the world. America was to feature last in the programme, and would be the most important series of performances. After months of touring, Stewart and the band would be in good form and able to excel.

Rod was pleased with the new album but he must have been disappointed with the rather lukewarm initial response which it received from the musical papers. Every artist must suffer criticism from journals from time to time; even if it seems unjustified. By this stage in his career, Rod must now have a keen awareness of his own talent and remain relatively immune to cool reviews and barbed comment. He gives

Carmine Appice, Rod Stewart's drummer, was born in New York City. He played with Vanilla Fudge, a band with a progressive image. Carmine has known Rod since 1968 and, at one time, almost joined the Jeff Beck Group when Rod was vocalist. He did spend two years in the Beck, Bogart and Appice combo before joining Al Kooper, Barry Goldberg and Mike Oldfield in KGB. Appice says of Stewart 'Rod is the best singer in the world . . .'

John Jarvis, 22-year-old piano-player, is the band's youngest member. Born in Pasadena, California, Jarvis was signed to a publishing company by the time he was 15. He has played on albums for Art Garfunkel, Ringo Starr, Leo Sayer and Rod Stewart. Jarvis is a musician with a classical background and an extensive range of playing styles. Rod's band is the first professional band which he has been in 'I just never found a band I liked'.

Philip Chen, bass guitarist, comes from Kingston, Jamaica. He played with Jimmy James and the Vagabonds in the mid 1960s, developing his reggae-playing with the Vagabonds until leaving to take up studio work. When the opportunity to join Rod Stewart offered itself, Chen said that 'studio work wasn't much of a challenge anymore and I always liked Rod's singing, so it was natural'. 'I'm gonna devote all my time to Rod'.

---

the impression that reviews do not worry him and that he knows that the final critic is the record-buyer, who is not necessarily a reader of music papers. Certainly the radio stations, particularly those in America, gave endless tracking to Stewart's **A Night On The Town**, and the response strongly suggested that many more people were now listening to Rod Stewart's lyrics and enjoying his music.

Rod's choice of band was obviously important. Its personnel would clearly show where he thought that his first solo days would lead but at first, his plans were hidden from the press. It came into the open with the news that Rod was interviewing and auditioning guitarists and bass players. But there were no applicants for the band's drummer as Rod wanted Kenny Jones to join. Eventually, however, Jones decided against joining a new band which would be built up around Rod Stewart.

A Night On The Town was well promoted. A film about Rod was shown by a British independent television channel. A BBC film was also shown titled **Rod The Mod Comes of Age**. There was much interest in the song **The Killing Of Georgie** both from 'gay' communities and the national newspapers. The television programmes produced a variety of comments and criticism. His stage act, as portrayed by the independent television film, led to discussions about his sexuality which brought about a tidal wave of publicity. Some critics saw him prancing around on a stage with

what he himself agreed was certainly 'camp' gestures. In the British paper, *Gay News*, he said, 'I suppose I did come off a bit poofy. But I was tired of the person I had become with The Faces, tired of the person who didn't make very good albums.' What, the music papers wondered, did all this have to do with gutsy rock 'n' roll? Barbara Charone of *Sounds*, a British rock paper, asked Rod about the 'pin-up' photo portraits which were appearing. 'I like all that. It might look silly, but it makes me feel sensuous.' A few days later, Stewart showed some impatience with the music critics. He stated that if he was not on T.V. people said, why not? and if he was, they asked why? so, what could he do?

The BBC film documented Rod's various activities, over a period of time. Obviously, the programme was not planned to promote the album, but it was watched by a large audience and featured Rod as a talented singer-songwriter. The camera also caught a few awkward and embarrassing moments but it was an interesting study of how far Rod had progressed as an artist. The early days of his career strongly contrasted with his present jet-set image. There were scenes of Rod racing up to Scotland for football and enjoying drinks with his family. Some press reaction to the film was critical. Rod replied to his critics that he was just being honest. He said his fans knew that he made a great deal of money, and he was tired of people who made a lot of money and then tried pleading poverty,

because they thought that being honest might harm their image.

Stewart was disappointed that the film only used one of his songs when eight hours of rehearsal had been filmed. As he told Rosalind Russell of *Record Mirror*, 'But with these programmes you're in the hands of the editor and producer'. However unsatisfactory both Rod and his critics found these films, they effectively brought the name Rod Stewart into households throughout Britain and doubtless increased his popularity.

Plans were announced in October of 1976 for a film, with Rod Stewart, Leo Sayer and British girl-singer Lynsey De Paul featured on the soundtrack. The film satirised World War Two and the music comprised a series of Beatle songs. The production was by Lou Reizner, who was responsible for **Tommy** and had, of course, been closely associated with Rod since his early solo days with Mercury records. It was planned that Rod's own British record label, Riva, would issue the film's soundtrack. One of Rod's songs was **Get Back** which, when issued as a single, became an instant hit. A special T.V. programme was also planned for Christmas Eve showing Stewart's concert at Olympia in London.

But even film and T.V. plans were over-shadowed by further news. This was the announcement of a Rod Stewart tour and definite news of the new band line-up. After a fairly long period without much action this news was greeted with great enthusiasm. Rod talked with considerable animation and expressed great confidence in the artists which he had selected. The band was named as Carmine Appice on drums; Jim Cregan, guitar; Gary Grainger, guitar; Phil Chen on bass; John Jarvis, piano and Billy Peek, guitar. Three of the musicians were British and three were from America. Stewart said that John Jarvis was the first band member to be selected. Steve Cropper had recommended him and he had also played on **A Night On The Town**. He had previously played piano on an Art Garfunkel solo album and worked with both Leo Sayer and Ringo Starr. Carmine Appice had been part of the Beck, Bogert, Appice Band, and known to Rod from the days of the Jeff Beck Group in the late 1960s. Billy Peek had been seen by Rod on an American T.V. **Midnight Special** with Chuck Berry. It appeared that Peek had been with the famous American artist for about seven years. He was from St. Louis in Missouri and had made five albums with Chuck Berry. Phil Chen was also known to Rod from the early days. At one point he was considered for The Faces line-up but he declined an offer to join, and eventually Tetsu Yamauchi became the bass player of the group. Phil Chen was from Jamaica, and his first experience of Britain was touring with Jimmy James and the Vagabonds in the mid-1960s. Chen was responsible for introducing reggae into the band and his work had included sessions with artists like Donovan, Johnny Nash, Beck, and Toots and the Maytals. It seemed that he was gradually getting tired of session bookings and was pleased at the prospect of being on the road and facing a live audience again. Jim Cregan was a familiar name to British fans and is married to singer Linda Lewis. He had been long associated with a number of successful bands, and had a strong reputation as a session artist. He had played with Taste, Rory Gallagher, Family and Steve Harley & Cockney Rebel. Gary Grainger had been with Strider who, at one time, had toured with The Faces.

Rod's new band had three guitarists. It was something that he had wanted for some years. He compared it to the original Fleetwood Mac line-up, and said that it had been in his mind ever since The Faces had been formed. It was also a group where everyone was capable of singing harmonies. Stewart wanted three guitars because he was able to place one at either side of the stage, and one in the middle which could surround the vocals.

Rod talked of getting the 'musical buzz' back and said that the band stood on its own, and was not a backing group. If he had wanted that, then he would have engaged people more closely associated with his recent recordings. In common with The Faces, he and the Band had a 'good-time' camaraderie

but there was no intention of giving the impression of being under-rehearsed or under-played. At their rehearsals the band sparkled and Stewart was enthusiastic. Tour dates were announced for the new Rod Stewart Band. The Band would spend three weeks in Scandinavia and Europe, then Britain, beginning with Manchester and following with dates which would take them into the New Year in Scotland. The band's first gig was in Norway on November 1. Barbara Charone was at Rod's Danish concert, and she said that through fourteen songs and an encore, the Rod Stewart Band mounted a continuous but well-paced assault. The show opened with **Three Time Loser** and then proceeded into **You Wear It Well**, **Big Bayou**, **Tonight's The Night**, **The Wild Side Of Life**, **This Old Heart Of Mine**, **Sweet Little Rock 'n' Roller**, **I Don't Want To Talk About It**, **Maggie May**, **Angel**, **You Keep Me Hangin' On**, **The Killing Of Georgie** and **I'm Losing You**. The last number was **Sailing** and the encore, appropriately, **Stay With Me**. The band wore rather exotic gear and Stewart was dressed in baggy red satin pants and a white satin shirt with matching jacket.

Famous for his style, Rod sets the trends with exotic clothes. Satins in particular are a favourite material and prove stunningly effective under the special stage lighting, focusing the audience's attention with their brilliant colours.

She said that Stewart was most excited at the way the band were playing and he was elated with his own singing. He was even now looking beyond Europe, Britain, Australasia toward America, his new homeland. Before an American tour, there would be a new album possibly to be recorded in Munich or even Canada. One thing was certain – Rod would soon be visiting America and he knew that he was assured of a marvellous welcome because of his recent record successes.

His Olympia Concert in London was a huge success. People liked the band and they liked Rod. Banished were the fears of how he would appear and how he would sing. The world of T.V.'s **Night On The Town** seemed far away. Rod now had experience and expertise and knew about audience and stage control. And it must have been exhilarating for him as he sang and heard the audience sing along with him. His fans swung their scarves and made lots of en-

thusiastic noise as they watched Rod pace up and down the large stage of Olympia, a building used more for exhibitions than rock concerts. Paul McCartney attended the concert together with Marc Bolan, Alvin Stardust and Gary Glitter.

Stewart was easily able to dominate the performance when he chose but at the same time it was obvious he respected his band. He allowed them the spotlight, he gave them time to let loose and develop their own playing. The three-guitar front line-up worked well and was, for the audience, an exciting musical event. But in addition there was a good pianist and bass-player combined with the power of Carmine Appice's drumming. Appice produced a veritable percussive storm but he also fitted in neatly with the

overall sound. He gave Stewart the right backbeat and there was precision in his playing. So often in bands the drummer, however skilled, can become rather colourless as an individual but with Appice, this was not so. At some points the audience broke into appreciative applause but the band also shouted praise. Jim Cregan looked cool on stage but played sizzling guitar. He was into the music and so were all the members of the group. Stewart had a highly professional Band. There were no real surprises in the choice of songs. When he sang his classic, **Maggie May**, he invited vocal contribution from the band and from the audience. Rod sang the encore **Stay With Me** from the top of the piano.

The British music press made ap-

proving noises, though one or two papers were naturally a little cautious. With what seemed to be one voice, they all urged Rod to keep his band together and some hoped there would be no battles within the group. It was thought that if everyone stayed together, The Rod Stewart Band could, very soon, join the ranks of popular music's all-time successful bands.

The road was not completely smooth for Rod, however. He developed a throat infection and there had to be changes made in the planning of the Scottish gigs. Also a minor hassle occurred with police when they raided the band's tour hotel in search of drugs. This somewhat marred the end of the highly successful tour.

In February 1977, a new single was

Rod thrills his audiences with his smokey-rich voice and the sensuous, restless movements of his stage performances.

issued by Rod in America. It was **First Cut Is The Deepest**, taken from his **A Night On The Town** album. The song was written by Cat Stevens and made popular in Britain during the late 1960s by a talented girl singer, P. P. Arnold. Rod's single immediately entered the Billboard Hot 100.

During the same month, Rod was touring in Australia. Several out-door concerts were cancelled owing to heavy rain but in spite of these set-backs Rod enjoyed a very enthusiastic reception. In April an album **The Best Of Rod And The Faces** was issued and Rod was

planning his next solo album and think-ing of the autumn and America.

Rod's new-found freedom and the keen response from his fans to his new band must have given Rod all the confi-dence which he needed to make a suc-cess of this new stage in his career. He had drawn together a talented group of musicians whom he could rely on to give him strong and sympathetic sup-port. The years with The Faces have given him the experience and know-ledge to understand his audiences and give them what they want: showman-ship, spectacle, earthiness and, above all, that special, smoky-rich voice which at times can be touching; but having such sensual overtones. The other side to his talents – that of composer – has yet to be fully developed. The sensitivity

and uniqueness of **The Killing Of Georgie** cannot be denied but he has yet to achieve his own personal classic. But it is certain that he will.

One other talent which Rod possesses is an ability which may guarantee him a lasting future as a singer. This is his talent for selecting song material which he can adapt for his own voice and style of presentation. He chooses good material which has perhaps been largely ignored and blends it, arranges it and, indelibly stamps it with his own per-sonality.

What makes an artist successful? It is a hard subject to analyse, but, looking at the combined talents of Rod Stewart it is possible that these are some of the ingredients which create the magic of a super-star.

'I'm all bunches of flowers' said Rod the Romantic. **Above:** Rod and Britt Ekland in the drawing room of Cranbourne Court, Windsor. **Left:** A photograph of Rod, on the steps of his private jet, taken by Britt. **Right:** Serious after-dinner conversation between Rod Stewart and Elton John.

Rod Stewart lives stylishly; owning elegant homes, giving champagne parties; chartering jets; ordering pairs of shoes by the half-dozen and spending enormous sums of money on having clothes specially designed for him. Rod may be a millionaire, but money is a subject which he declines to speak about. In Britain, however, there was a great deal of speculation about his income tax bill. Rod now spends most of his time at his American home or travelling the world with Britt Ekland on tour with his own band, which took to the road during the early winter of 1976.

Rod Stewart's present success as an artist is far removed from the days when he began singing with John Baldry for a small weekly wage. It may have been a chance meeting with John Baldry on Twickenham railway station, but Rod had ambition and he was determined to reach the top. Speaking of the money and property which he has achieved he says: 'I've earned everything myself. I've worked hard for it'.

Much publicity has been given to Rod's homes. The first house he bought was near his parents' home, situated in Highgate in north London. His second house was more spacious, though Rod called it plain with insufficient space for a studio or rehearsal room.

His third and most famous home was the magnificent country house, Cranbourne Court near Windsor which he bought in 1971. His bank balance had benefited from three top selling solo albums and hit singles like **Maggie May**, which had topped both British and American charts.

The property was close to the famed Windsor Castle and also Windsor Great Park which had been the location for several free rock music festivals. Helped by girlfriend Dee Harrington, Rod spent two years decorating and lavishly furnishing its spacious interior. It consisted of thirty two rooms, including eight bedrooms, five bathrooms and six receptions rooms, a large stable block, rooms for servants and a lodge. It also possessed a superb swimming pool and extensive grounds totalling 14 acres. Into this massive Georgian mansion, Rod introduced his own particular interests. He decorated one of his walls with photographs of Denis Law in action; he installed a king-size bed with its bedcover featuring the rich colour of the Scottish lion, a motif which appeared throughout the house in many forms. There was a snooker or pool room which housed Rod's collection of gold discs. Antique and reproduction furniture filled the house and huge French advertising posters decorated some of the reception rooms.

When Rod left Britain to settle in the U.S.A. he put his Windsor home up for sale. He then moved into a modest house which he rented in Beverley Hills, while Britt lived in a much more affluent residence in the Bel Air location. However, Rod was preparing his own sumptuous residence, built in the style of a French chateau. One British paper has called it a 'tax-exile's dream'.

One of Rod's keenest interests is collecting and driving beautiful and unusual autos. He has owned such exotic machines as Lamborghinis, Mercedes, Ferraris, Excalibers and Panthers. A 1932 Rolls Royce has also featured in his collection. He is interested in the maintenance of his cars and, in fact, once built his own Marcos sports model.

And yet for all his riches, property and possessions, Rod Stewart has obviously maintained a control over his life and affairs. Having satisfied his desire to have all the possessions which he used to dream of owning, Rod states quite simply, 'Peace and quiet . . . it's what I've worked for,' and also, 'I enjoy spending but I don't waste it . . . there are times when I've got long pockets and short arms.' And there are also reports of Rod welcoming fans into his homes, if they can find their location. At times he likes having drinks in bars and pubs and eating in small, cheap restaurants as much as joining in with the 'jet-set'. He also enjoys chatting to people and has said, 'You gotta keep in touch with the people you're making records for . . . whether it's just to boost my ego . . . I don't know . . . I need to do it. I enjoy it, anyway.'

Stewart, man of property and wealth, is also a person who identifies closely with his public. Beautiful women, champagne and fast cars feature in the life of the super-star, but Scotland, football and his fans are a very important part of Rod's life. This is part of the reason why Rod Stewart has become one of the most successful artists and stars on the music scene today.

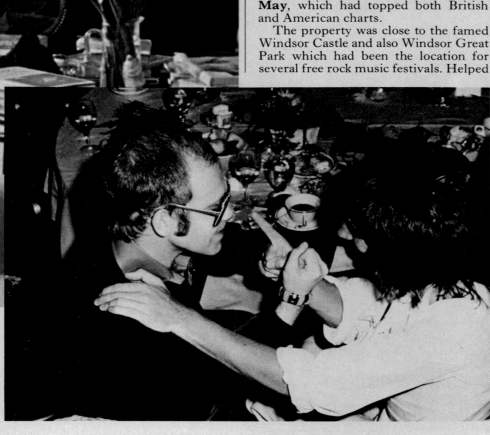

The Trendsetter

In November, 1976, Rod said, 'I'm in a position to be able to change as I feel like it.' And change is certainly what Rod is all about. His ability to switch from one musical style to another is well accepted. He can appear to be all things to all fans. In February 1971, Chris Welch of *Melody Maker* said of Rod: 'Quite how he has managed to satisfy, simultaneously, the English craze for soccer, the Scottish need for tartan, the gay world's need for glamour, the rock world's lust for glory and the public's love of foppery is a tribute to his shrewd chameleon qualities.'

Rosalind Russell of *Record Mirror* described him as looking more like a Christmas tree when she met Rod in London. He wore bright green velvet jeans, sported a red Inca sweater, leg warmers, red scarf and a furry possum jacket. He told her he had no spare tyre around the midriff and his weight was $10\frac{1}{2}$ stone, which corresponded with his weight when he was a mere 18. He also said that he had dyed his hair red to look good under the stage lighting.

Even back in the days of the Hoochie Coochie Men, Rod was famous for his style. He dressed sharply in the 'mod' manner and in fact achieved the nickname 'Rod the Mod'. He has always had a knack for dressing in an eye-catching way – a talent which was to establish him as a trendsetter. The 'Mod' days, of the R & B movement in the mid-1960s, saw the arrival of patterned trousers, velvets and satins, coloured shoes, bright vegetable dyes and a general camp and gaiety which

Left: A red-headed Rod looking far ahead in leg-warmers, Inca sweater and possum jacket. **Right:** By complete contrast, a smoothly elegant Stewart looking tall and sleek in cream satin. **Below:** Earlier days in patterns and checks outside his Windsor home.

preceded the era of boutiques. Rod was part of such a scene. Satin has always been a favourite material and he likes mixing bright colours with black.

He has never worn what the magazines consider to be the style of the moment and rarely, if ever, has he been photographed by a magazine or journal to model clothes. He chooses his own style of dress. Usually he is flamboyant and extravagant in his choice of clothes and colours, though on occasion he has developed a liking for dark colours. Some people have described Rod as a 'poser' while others have called him vain. Whatever the case, he does spend enormous sums of money on clothes and considerable time ensuring that his appearance, his hair in particular, is the way he wants it.

In later days, the word 'camp' has often been applied to Rod, particularly because of his stage posturing with his famous strut. He has been a trendsetter for young men but has much influenced the girls, who have adapted many of his fashions for their own use.

Rod has always insisted that he does not choose especially extravagant clothes for the stage, but clothes which he would equally well wear during the day or when relaxing at home. He says that people see the 'real Rod', whatever the situation, and comments that though some people find his dress colourful, he doesn't see it as outrageous or weird. He says they could be worn by anyone. He sees himself more as a casual dresser than someone concerned with what he calls 'the smart stuff'.

In 1973 he moved through the American concert scene wearing, among other items, a baby blue pant-suit, yellow negligeé, gold toreador pants, white sleeveless top and flowered muffler. In Britain, during 1976 he caused consternation in some quarters, even among his admirers, with his appearance on a British T.V. film, **Night On The Town**. Rosalind Russell said in *Record Mirror*, November 13, that the film featured 'a lot of shots of interesting anatomical detail'. Rod said it was very camp and it came out very schmaltzy, but remarked that people should have seen him that morning when he had been playing football, squelching around in ankle-deep mud!

One of Britain's respected show-business columnists, Judith Simons of the *Daily Express*, described Rod on the 1976 U.K. tour as akin to a marauder from the East, less the scimitar. He wore red silk harem trousers with a bare midriff exposed by a white silk shirt. She commented that he looked more akin to a 'strident football supporter in fancy dress than anything else'. Whatever the pros and cons and opinions of Rod's clothing, sexuality and exhibitionism, one thing remains constant. For his fans, both male and female, Rod is *the* trendsetter though sometimes he is too 'far-out' for them to follow.

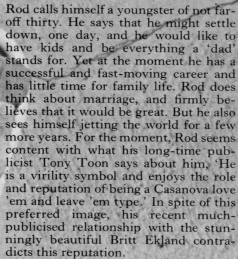

Rod's Girls

Rod calls himself a youngster of not far-off thirty. He says that he might settle down, one day, and he would like to have kids and be everything a 'dad' stands for. Yet at the moment he has a successful and fast-moving career and has little time for family life. Rod does think about marriage, and firmly believes that it would be great. But he also sees himself jetting the world for a few more years. For the moment, Rod seems content with what his long-time publicist Tony Toon says about him, 'He is a virility symbol and enjoys the role and reputation of being a Casanova love 'em and leave 'em type.' In spite of this preferred image, his recent much-publicised relationship with the stunningly beautiful Britt Ekland contradicts this reputation.

Rod has been seen and photographed with numerous lovely girls, including Paulene Stone, wife of the late Laurence Harvey, Joanna Lumley, Susan George, model Kathy Simmonds and Princess Meriam of Johore. The newspaper gossip writers were even excited into romantic prose with whispers of a relationship with ex-American President Ford's daughter, Susan. His longest relationship, to date, has been with an English model, Dee Harrington, who shared Rod's magnificent house, Cranbourne Court, near Windsor, England. Rod bought horses for her and together they spent months shopping for furniture and art-works for their home. The relationship became so important to Rod that in New York during 1971, he announced that they were engaged. The wedding never took place, however, and they finally parted. Rod told Tony Toon, 'Dee and I had a good run, but we hadn't got a written contract, requiring six months notice.' Dee was considerably upset and she jetted across the Atlantic. But when she saw him in a Los Angeles club with Britt, she left and said that she wished to preserve what was left of her dignity.

No-one apart from Rod himself knows how serious his relationships were with the various beautiful girls whom he has been seen out with. Model Kathy Simmonds said that the evenings which she spent with Rod were fabulous. Kathy said Rod was someone who could be trusted and was faithful to his word. Her view on Rod is that one day he will make a serious commitment and keep to it. She said she was not possessive and nobody owned Rod.

Rod is always followed around by a bevy of girls. Particularly in America, Rod's fans want to be with their favourite star. Some groups have been involved with stories connected with their hotel and travel activities, but Rod and The Faces have never featured in this kind of gossip. At most, columnists have seen Rod's stage act akin to 'total erotica', but that is all.

Rod surprised many British people during 1976 by being interviewed by *Gay News*, a magazine for male homosexuals. The topicality of this doubtless stemmed from his multi-million selling disc, **The Killing Of Georgie**, a song which told of one of Rod's friends who was prevented from finding out the true nature of his sexuality by an intolerant society. Rod denied that he had ever had a homosexual relationship but said that he had an enormous sexual drive. He called himself a romantic, 'I'm all bunches of flowers'. Certainly his relationship with Britt Ekland has had a romantic aura. Rod has said, 'I won't look at any other woman other than Britt'. It is an affair which has fascinated the rock and popular press. Initially some thought it was just another Rod flirtation and they waited for it to end and for Rod to become fancy-free again. Rod has had no doubts about their affair, however, and on one occasion even left his treasured address book behind when he flew out to join Britt in Los Angeles. His chauffeur Cyril took charge of the volume and Rod said, 'He's 68 so it should be safe with him'. He has talked of Britt causing major changes in his life and that now he has no interest in other women. When asked about Rod's activities Britt told Britain's *Daily Mirror*, 'The only time he hurt me was when he told the newspapers, before mentioning it to me, that he didn't think he'd marry me.'

The couple share a house in Los Angeles's Holmby Hills area. Britt is slightly older than Rod; she is 34 and he 32, but hardly old enough to qualify in the context of a remark that Rod once made that he really liked older women. One of the oddest stories surrounding the couple goes back to a post-concert party when Bob Dylan and his wife turned up, and he and Rod agreed to have a jam together. It seems Dylan went off to tune his guitar but Rod was so preoccupied with Britt that he completely forgot.

By mid-1977 the two were still together even though it has been said that romances cannot last in show business. Perhaps Rod and Britt will prove that statement false.

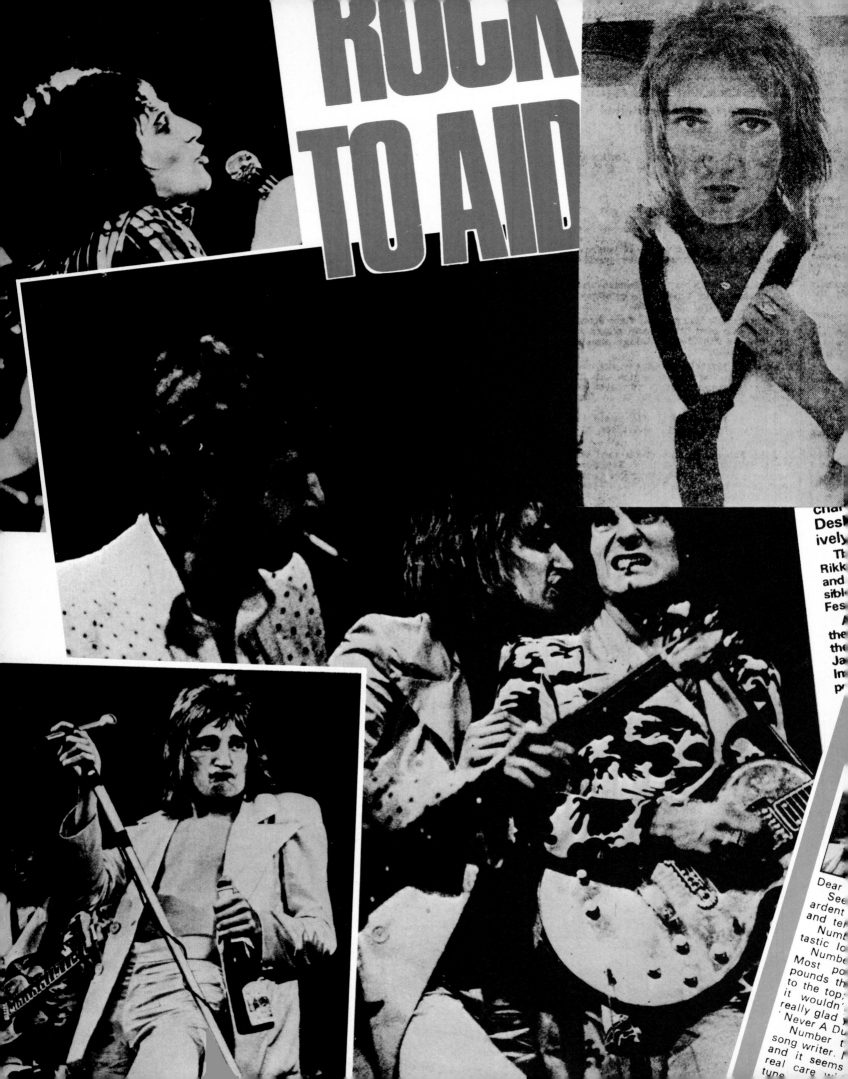

ROCK TO AID

Hitting the Headlines

For an interested public, Rod Stewart provides a constant stream of lively news. Newspaper and magazine headlines relating to Rod are dramatic and bold, so too is their supporting copy. *Circus* magazine of March, 1972 proclaimed, 'Flashman: Stewart at the Pub – Rod Stewart spins into the room like a roadrunner caught in a wind tunnel and spills the strategy that's made him The Face among the Faces'. *Sounds*, for November 6, 1976, headlined across two pages, 'The Redeeming Of Rod' which they followed with copy relating to the trials and tribulations of being a rock 'n' roll star with an identity problem. Below the central photograph, a quote from Rod read, 'I can't win anymore. I can't do a bloody thing right'. *Rolling Stone*'s writer Tom Nolan accompanied Rod and The Faces for their 1975 finale in the States, 'Rod Stewart Faces the American Dream – A Solo Spotlight, a Hollywood Mansion, a Glamorous Girlfriend and Lower Taxes. . . . Every Picture Tells A Story, Don't It?' A less original headline was, 'Rod – Rags to Riches' coined by the British teen magazine, *Music Star*. They add, 'Rod Stewart was brought up in an ordinary house in North London – now he lives in a right royal palace. We went to see him. . . .' 'Face is Familiar', said Britain's *Western Daily Press*, Bristol, on December 3, 1973, while the British journal, *Music Scene*, printed 'Rod Stewart – Rock United'. *Record Mirror* of November 1976 referred to 'Red Rod – the many phases and colours of Rod Stewart'.

Other newspaper and magazine headlines have been less concerned with making puns on record titles and the names, and more interested in relating to a specific aspect of Rod or The Faces. Even Rock star, Patti Smith's article was given the headline, however, by the New York, *Metropolitan Review*, January 1972, 'Rod Stewart; Just Another Face'. In April 1976, *New Musical Express* said, ''Ere, Rod . . . Wot Abaht the workers then?', while for culture, U.K.'s *Melody Maker* of April 14, 1973 celebrated a Faces' album release (the reception of which should have been in Paris), by appealing to its bi-lingual readership with 'Les Faces – C'est très NEAT'. On other occasions the headline has been weak with most attention directed toward what is usually a quote from Rod. The *New Musical Express* of August 12, 1972, headlined, A Question of Flash, but more relevant was Rod's quote, 'I think England is a little fed up with its stars being humble'. The *Melody Maker* for April 21, 1972 put 'Rod' into block letters and then ran down the page, 'Our new album is a disgrace . . . a bloody mess'. Rod appeared on the front-page of Britain's multi-million selling, *Radio Times* (which features national radio and T.V.

programmes). The journal printed 'Rock and Rod' and then a stream of words, 'Rod Stewart once dreamed of playing soccer for Scotland, but he has become one of the other great heroes of our time – a pop singer. From his working-class origins to his tax exile in Los Angeles, he's an almost archetypal rock star'.

Obviously the press has created many of the headlines and articles around Rod's enjoyment of female company and, recently, his love for Britt Ekland. The British *Daily Mirror* headlines 'My Life with Rod – By Britt Ekland', and later 'My Guilt' and 'The Only Girl for Me' provide headlines for the *Daily Mirror*'s serialized *Rod Stewart Story*. A typical pun-filled double-page-spread in the British *News of the World*, dated June 8, 1975, proclaims 'Hot Rod's Sexy Life at the Top' and in various sub-headings spread in boxes on the pages, 'Britt brings about the taming of the Stew' plus 'Next Week – The girls Hot Rod left behind'. When Rod met Britt the London *Daily Express* said, 'Every picture tells a story . . . as rock star Rod shows off Britt, the new love in his life' and with larger type-face there followed, 'It's just a game says "jilted" Dee'. On December 16, 1976, the *Lancashire Evening Telegraph* asked, 'Has Britt tamed Rod the raver? – Albert Watson meets a puzzling rock star'. Nor has Rod's obvious passion for Scotland and football escaped the attention of the Press. When Scotland drew with West Germany in November of 1973, *Glasgow's Evening Citizen*, headlined a whole page, 'Scotland's Super Fans!' – 'What a night for pop kings Rod and Elton . . . and what a gift for the "Lawman". It called them the 'self-appointed footballing groupies'. The music press has caught Rod training with Elton and pictured them on a football field on a cold November day. The press has also found Rod playing with show-biz teams and report that he plays football with considerable skill. A major moment in Rod's life was reported by Britain's *Sports Mail*, of August 1, 1976. A headline read, 'Day Superscot Rod Got His First Cap'. A veterans' charity game had been organised between two sides, Scottish Select and an English side. Rod played for the former and distinguished himself amongst some, now retired, star players. After the game, Rod got his first Scottish cap, a tartan tammie!

Apart from general coverage of album issues, usually found in the music press, few of Rod's interests have been featured by the press. Rod hit the headlines again, however, when he became

Hot Rod in a Blaze of Publicity. Rod Stewart's successful career and glamorous life-style constantly features on the pages of the international popular press and music papers.

interested in politics during 1976. When the press realised that Britain's Liberal party leader, David Steel, was a 'Stewart fan' it was inevitable that the headline would appear, 'Pop around to the House, David Steel asks "Lib" Rod' (*Daily Mail*, October 28, 1976). David Steel met Rod for dinner in Beverly Hills and for lunch at the House of Commons, London, home of Britain's Parliament.

Rod once said he would be upset if he thought all the press coverage of him prevented people from finding out about his music. He has, however, been unable to avoid the constant press and film coverage. And according to at least one British pop photographer, Ian Dickson, he must be the most photographed pop personality and possibly the most accessible. Certainly, Rod's home and cars, his fashion and girls are ideal for the press photographer who wants variety and interest in his photographs. Rod Stewart's musical talent has rarely interested the popular press, except for reports about long queues for concert tickets the night prior to the opening of box-offices or features about fans being unable to obtain tickets. The *West Lancashire Evening Gazette* quoted one fan: 'We would only do it for The Faces. They're the best band in the world, and we want the best seats to see them from'.

Rod was featured in a British magazine, *New Statesman* in its issue of December 1976. The copy was headed 'This Old Heart Of His'. It named Rod as one of the most versatile singers to emerge in recent years. It suggested that Rod's single **Killing of Georgie** caught the artist's dual nature for, on the A-side was Rod playing the aggressive degenerate – on the B-side Rod appears as the naive romantic. Rod has also been featured in the BBC magazine *The Listener*. The writer was the producer of a special TV documentary which had been made about Rod for the series, Omnibus, shown on BBC Television. Like most famous artists, Rod has suffered criticism from his public. Some have accused Rod of 'selling-out' and expressed puzzlement at the showbiz, super-star image given expression by the popular press. At moments during his career, letter writers have said that Rod was slipping in his musical ability. Indeed, Rod has regretted certain periods of his life, times when he felt that the music was lost among the activities of the band and general Faces fun and games.

Apart from covering sensational stories of Rod Stewart's life-style, the press have produced some lively reviews

Left: Rod is interviewed by Melvin Bragg for a BBC TV documentary *Rod The Mod Comes Of Age*. The interview took place on London's River Thames and the Houses of Parliament can be seen in the background.

and comment on the artist's work. Jon Landau, for the American publication, *The Real Paper*, July 4, 1973, commented, when reviewing with the Stewart compendium, *Play It Again Rod*: 'As good as the near genius who made it, an exciting record to play, excessive in both the right and wrong ways, and above all, an impressive testament to the classiness and character of one of rock's five leading men'. When Landau came to comment on the track, **Twistin' The Night Away**, he added, 'It is everything Rod Stewart means to me – sentiment, even beery-eyed nostalgia, but a hard, tough, instinctive feeling for the place in the rock pantheon'. In Britain's *Daily Mirror*, February 17, 1977, Bill Hagerty writes, 'The enormous sales of Stewart's **A Night On The Town** album, closely followed by a stunningly successful European and British tour, have placed him unequivocally among the top half-dozen rock performers in the world'.

Rod will undoubtedly continue to feature in the pages of papers and provide a subject of interest for his fans and people in the music business. In a rather weary musical world, devoid of incident and personality, Rod Stewart produces a vibrant burst of colour and interest.

Stewart himself has remained fairly quiet about his views of the press reaction to him. His most vociferous moments have been at times when he feels himself trapped into endless interviews which, for the most part, year in and year out, have the interviewers

asking the same questions. He is constantly asked about his teen days, the first bands and experiences, even though he has gone on record endless times with his responses. And likewise, he has also been caught in somewhat off moments by some reporters clamouring for interviews after a long and exhausting concert. One such incident was recorded in the *Los Angeles Free Press*, October 26, 1973 where Clayton Frohman had the task of interviewing Rod who, on the previous evening had badly cut his foot when he had kicked an amplifier. Clayton tells of a P.R. girl pleading with Rod to give him a few minutes and then finally the singer agreed. Clayton found himself on a spot when Rod told him he hated interviews and answering the same questions. Eventually the interview did proceed and sympathy must lie with both, for different reasons.

In an interview Rod gave with Barbara Charone in the issue of *Rolling Stone*, for January 13, 1977, the singer said that he would dread to think that he sold records because Britt and himself were featured on page three of the Evening Whatever. Yet, at the same time, he is shrewd enough to know that all publicity can, if carefully handled, be beneficial. Since his recording of **Sailing** became a hit in Britain, he knows that his buying audience has widened enormously and they are not necessarily the people who read the musical press. Their interest is aroused by articles in the popular press which feature his personality and exciting lifestyle.

Football, one of the loves of Rod's life, provides him with relaxation and enjoyment. **Far right:** Stewart poses with the Goaldiggers at Harlow, England. To the left of Rod is broadcaster Michael Parkinson and on the right is singer-songwriter Elton John.

Ron Wood.

SINGLES

GOOD MORNING LITTLE SCHOOLGIRL / I'M GONNA MOVE TO THE OUTSKIRTS OF TOWN (1964, Decca).

THE DAY WILL COME / WHY DOES IT GO ON (1965, Columbia).

SHAKE / I JUST GOT SOME (1966, Columbia).

I COULD FEEL THE WHOLE WORLD TURN ROUND / CURTAINS (instrumental). A single released by Shotgun Express (1966, Columbia).

LITTLE MISUNDERSTOOD / SO MUCH TO SAY (1968, Immediate).

HANDBAGS AND GLADRAGS / MAN OF CONSTANT SORROW (1970, Mercury).

IN A BROKEN DREAM / DOING FINE. A single recorded with Python Lee Jackson (1970, Youngblood).

MAGGIE MAY / REASON TO BELIEVE. This single reached number one position in both U.K. and U.S.A. charts (1971, Mercury).

YOU WEAR IT WELL / LOST PARAGUAYOS (1972, Mercury).

ANGEL / WHAT MADE MILWAUKEE FAMOUS (HAS MADE A LOSER OUT OF ME) (1972, Mercury).

OH NO, NOT MY BABY / JODIE (1973, Mercury).

FAREWELL / BRING IT ON HOME TO ME – YOU SEND ME (1974, Mercury).

IT'S ALL OVER NOW / HANDBAGS AND GLADRAGS (1975, Mercury).

SAILING / STONE COLD SOBER (1975, Warner Brothers).

THIS OLD HEART OF MINE / ALL IN THE NAME OF ROCK 'N' ROLL (1975, Riva).

SKYE BOAT SONG / SKYE BOAT SONG (instrumental) (1976, Riva).

TONIGHT'S THE NIGHT / THE BALL TRAP (1976, Riva).

THE KILLING OF GEORGIE / FOOL FOR YOU (1976, Riva).

SAILING / STONE COLD SOBER (re-released in the U.K. when adopted as the title music in a British T.V. series).

GET BACK / TRADE WINDS (1976, Riva).

MAGGIE MAY / YOU WEAR IT WELL / TWISTIN' THE NIGHT AWAY (1976, Mercury).

FIRST CUT IS THE DEEPEST / I DON'T WANT TO TALK ABOUT IT (1977, Riva).

SINGLES RECORDED WITH OTHER ARTISTS

The Jeff Beck Group

YOU'LL BE MINE / UP ABOVE MY HEAD. Stewart duets (uncredited) with Baldry on the B-side (1964, United Artists).

TALLYMAN / ROCK MY PLIMSOUL. Stewart sings on the B-side but he is uncredited (1967, Columbia).

LOVE IS BLUE / I'VE BEEN DRINKING. Stewart sings (uncredited) on B-side (1968, Columbia).

The Faces

FLYING / THREE BUTTON HAND ME DOWN (1970, Warner Brothers).

HAD ME A REAL GOOD TIME / REAR WHEEL SKID (1970, Warner Brothers).

STAY WITH ME / DEBRIS (1972, Warner Brothers).

CINDY INCIDENTALLY / SKEWIFF (MEND THE FUSE) (1973, Warner Brothers).

DISHEVELMENT BLUES / (special flexi give-away-disc with British pop paper, *New Musical Express*).

POOLHALL RICHARD / I WISH IT WOULD RAIN (1973, Warner Brothers).

CINDY INCIDENTALLY / MEMPHIS / STAY WITH ME / POOLHALL RICHARD (maxi-single, 1974, Warner Brothers).

YOU CAN MAKE ME DANCE SING OR ANYTHING / AS LONG AS YOU TELL HIM (1974, Warner Brothers).

Model Faces created by Edwin Bellchamber for the album sleeve of **A Nod's As Good As A Wink To A Blind Horse**.

ALBUMS RECORDED WITH JEFF BECK

Truth (1968, Columbia) tracks: SHAPES OF THINGS / LET ME LOVE YOU / MORNING DEW / YOU SHOOK ME / OL' MAN RIVER / GREENSLEEVES / ROCK MY PLIMSOUL / BECK'S BOLERO / BLUES DE LUXE / I AIN'T SUPERSTITIOUS.

Beck Ola (1969, Columbia) tracks: ALL SHOOK UP / SPANISH BOOTS / GIRL FROM MILL VALLEY / JAILHOUSE ROCK / PLYNTH (WATER DOWN THE DRAIN) / THE HANGMAN'S KNEE / RICE PUDDING.

Comment

Stewart has said that he thought that both albums were good, describing the first as a 'real hallmark'. On the first album, only Beck's name appears on the front. The musicians are credited in small print on the back cover. Mickie Most is credited for the production of **Truth** with Jeff Beck receiving a credit for the arrangement. Rod has frequently disputed these two credits and maintains that the album was a team effort. **Truth** was not well received by Al Kooper, the reviewer of the American journal, *Rolling Stone*. Beck, himself saw the record as something of a 'hotch-potch' thrown together with little planning. Stewart, however, regards the record as contemporary blues and worthy of respect. Two of the tracks, 'You Shook Me' and 'I Ain't Superstitious' were by Willie Dixon.

    Beck Ola was recorded in 1969 and clearly showed a change in band emphasis from blues to somewhat crude 'heavy metal' music. Two of the tracks 'Jailhouse Rock' and 'All Shook Up' were Presley revivals. Emphasis was upon the instrumental backing.

ALBUMS RECORDED WITH THE FACES

First Step (1970, Warner Brothers) tracks:
WICKED MESSENGER / DEVOTION / SHAKE, SHUDDER, SHIVER / STONE / AROUND THE PLYNTH / FLYING / PINEAPPLE AND THE MONKEY / NOBODY KNOWS / LOOKING OUT THE WINDOW / THREE BUTTON HAND ME DOWN.

Long Player (1971, Warner Brothers) tracks:
BAD 'N' RUIN / TELL EVERYONE / SWEET LADY MARY / RICHMOND / MAYBE I'M AMAZED / HAD ME A REAL GOOD TIME / ON THE BEACH / I FEEL SO GOOD / JERUSALEM.

A Nod's As Good As A Wink To A Blind Horse (1972, Warner Brothers) tracks:
MISS JUDY'S FARM / YOU'RE SO RUDE / LOVE LIVED HERE / LAST ORDERS PLEASE / STAY WITH ME / DEBRIS / MEMPHIS / TOO BAD / THAT'S ALL YOU NEED.

Ooh La La (1973, Warner Brothers) tracks:
SILICONE GROWN / CINDY INCIDENTALLY / FLAGS AND BANNERS / MY FAULT / BORSTAL BOYS / FLY IN THE OINTMENT / IF I'M ON THE LATE SIDE / GLAD AND SORRY / JUST ANOTHER HONKY / OOH LA LA.

Coast To Coast Overture And Beginners (1974, Mercury) tracks:
IT'S ALL OVER NOW / CUT ACROSS SHORTY / TOO BAD / EVERY PICTURE TELLS A STORY / ANGEL / STAY WITH ME / I WISH IT WOULD RAIN / I'D RATHER GO BLIND / BORSTAL BOYS / AMAZING GRACE / JEALOUS GUY.

Snakes And Ladders (1976, Warners. U.S.A. only) tracks:
POOL HALL RICHARD / CINDY INCIDENTALLY / OOH LA LA / SWEET LADY MARY / FLYING / PINEAPPLE AND THE MONKEY / YOU CAN MAKE ME DANCE SING OR ANYTHING / HAVE ME A REAL GOOD TIME / STAY WITH ME / MISS JUDY'S FARM / SILICONE GROWN / AROUND THE PLYNTH.

The Best Of The Faces (1977, Riva. U.K. only) tracks:
FLYING / AROUND THE PLYNTH / NOBODY KNOWS / THREE BUTTON HAND ME DOWN / SWEET LADY MARY / MAYBE I'M AMAZED / HAD ME A REAL GOOD TIME / MISS JUDY'S FARM / MEMPHIS / TOO BAD / STAY WITH ME / THAT'S ALL YOU NEED / CINDY INCIDENTALLY / OOH LA LA / FLAGS AND BANNERS / BORSTAL BOYS / I WISH IT WOULD RAIN / POOL HALL RICHARD / YOU CAN MAKE ME DANCE SING OR ANYTHING / IT'S ALL OVER NOW.

Comment

The Faces albums tended to be overshadowed by Rod's solo discs. **A Nod's As Good As A Wink To A Blind Horse** did, however, receive considerable attention and critical acclaim. It may have benefited from the change of emphasis from Wood–Lane compositions to the Stewart–Wood partnership.

    First Step was issued in February 1970, which coincided with the release, by Mercury, of Rod's first solo album. **An Old Raincoat Won't Ever Let You Down**. The critics and feature-writers tended to devote more of their space to Rod's solo album than to **First Step**.

    First Step has a fairly loose style having only one track shorter than four minutes and many longer than five minutes. It gave more of an impression of individual styles rather than focusing the group as a whole. Stewart, was particularly interested in Dylan compositions and delivered 'Wicked Messenger' very forcefully. He was later to feature Dylan on his solo albums, **Every Picture Tells A Story**, **Smiler**, **Gasoline Alley** and **Never A Dull Moment**.

    Long Player was released in March, 1971 and it included Stewart's version

of the McCartney composition 'Maybe I'm Amazed' with Ronnie Lane singing the first verse. The song was re-recorded by The Faces as a single. The re-recording utilised the skills of James Taylor's engineer, Bill Lazarus, who double-tracked Ronnie's voice and shortened the instrumental break. The re-recording never appeared, however, in spite of enthusiasm shown by Stewart. The tracks for **Long Player** were made at various locations. 'Bad 'n' Ruin' and 'Tell Everyone' were recorded on The Rolling Stones Mobile Unit. Originally Morgan Studios, London, was the planned starting point for the album but things did not work out well and the Mobile was hired. The two live tracks from a recording at Fillmore East were also included which were 'Maybe I'm Amazed' and a Bill Broonzy number, 'I Feel So Good'. 'Had Me A Real Good Time' contributed to The Faces' now established image of being a reckless, hard-drinking kind of group. Ronnie Lane sang a solo number 'Richmond' and, with Wood, he sang 'On The Beach'. Rod, however, was gradually taking over as the focal point of The Faces. During an interview with *Zig Zag* magazine, Stewart expressed his opinion that the group needed a pro-

ducer for its next album. This led to the album **A Nod's As Good As A Wink To A Blind Horse**, being produced by Glyn Johns. This was later regarded by many music critics as one of The Faces' most successful albums. John Pidgeon, author and broadcaster, has termed it 'a model of rock and roll discipline' in his book *Rod Stewart and the Changing Faces*, 1976.

Part of its success can be attributed to the band's feeling that a first-class album was now necessary, following the disappointing reaction to the previous two. Rod said that he wished for a classic Faces' album and thought that they were trying too hard. He said that the band had never really been conscious of their group identity when recording and nor had they captured the atmosphere of their live concerts on disc. He thought that individual members were pushing their own styles too hard and he, too, was a guilty partner. The album's success coincided with that of Rod's third album, **Every Picture Tells A Story** and the two singles, 'Maggie May' and 'Stay With Me'. The Faces, at last, were making an impact upon the British public. The lyric strength of the album **A Nod's As Good As A Wink To A Blind Horse**

came from its succession of songs dealing with ordinary subjects and familiar attitudes which their audiences could identify with. 'Debris' and 'Love Lived Here' showed The Faces' more sensitive side but basically the album's music had fire and guts. The album reached number two in the British charts and the single from it, 'Stay With Me', reached number six. In the U.S.A. it was not so successful but it did reach number 17 position and remained in the Top 20 for about four weeks.

Ooh La La, the fourth album, was a chart success. A single was released from the album, 'Cindy Incidentally', which reached number two position in the British charts. Even when the single had finally dropped from the charts, there was still no release of **Ooh La La**. It finally appeared, however, and went to the top of the charts but unfortunately this success was short-lived, for within a month it had disappeared completely from the best-selling lists. This was perhaps due to the fact that the album was not entirely representative of The Faces as a whole. In parts it was melodic and pleasant, but for The Faces' fan, it was perhaps too soft and gentle, and lacked irreverence and guts. Some of its weakness arose because the band tended to wander into the studio and compose there and then, rather than preparing material in advance. There were also frequent disagreements between Rod and other members of the band about presentation.

Rod surprisingly issued a fiery set of criticisms of the album during interviews. *Melody Maker* ran his thoughts as an article headline, 'Rod: Our new album is a disgrace . . . a bloody mess'. The cut 'Borstal Boys' annoyed him more than most. He said the group couldn't play it, and he named one of the best tracks as 'Ooh la la' on which he didn't sing.

At the time, Rod said he was looking forward to making his own album. People began to wonder about Rod's future with The Faces. He told *Melody Maker*, however, in answer to the question of whether he thought more about his future than The Faces, 'Er . . . oh no. We're together for life.'

The album, **Coast To Coast Overture and Beginners** appeared on Mercury in the U.K. and on the Warner Brothers label in America, because of a dispute over Stewart's contract. The title bore the names, Rod Stewart/Faces. It was a typical Faces collection featuring among its tracks 'Amazing Grace' and Lennon's 'Jealous Guy'. Though there were many fans who obviously enjoyed the disc it suffered from criticism by the music papers. Group member Ian McLagan passionately defended it but the other Faces tended to dismiss it. To some listeners it had all the symptoms of a good band going through a bad time.

ROD STEWART SOLO ALBUMS

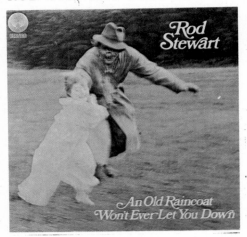

An Old Raincoat Won't Ever Let You Down (1970, Vertigo) tracks: STREET FIGHTING MAN / MAN OF CONSTANT SORROW / BLIND PRAYER / HANDBAGS AND GLADRAGS / AN OLD RAINCOAT WON'T EVER LET YOU DOWN / I WOULDN'T EVER CHANGE A THING / CINDY'S LAMENT / DIRTY OLD TOWN.

This album was titled for American release as **The Rod Stewart Album**. Rod Stewart said of this first album, 'I was very pleased with it when we finished, and I still am'. John Morthland, writing in *Rolling Stone*, said that it was magnificent, and expanded this by saying that, whether the song was a hard rocker, a soft ballad, or even an old folkblues, Rod triumphed in each of his eight tracks. Obviously Rod's track-selection is an interesting one. 'Street Fighting Man', a Jagger-Richard composition can be heard on the Stones' album, **Get Yer Ya-Yas Out**. Rod's folk roots were shown in his selection of Ewan McColl's 'Dirty Old Town' and the traditional song, 'Man Of Constant Sorrow'. Mike D'Abo ex-lead singer of Manfred Mann, contributed 'Handbags And Gladrags' which was later chosen for the B-side of 'It's All Over Now'. Four songs are credited to Rod Stewart. On the instrumental side, Stewart used Faces' members Ron Wood on bass and guitars and Ian MacLagan on organ.

Gasoline Alley (1970, Vertigo) tracks: GASOLINE ALLEY / IT'S ALL OVER NOW / ONLY A HOBO / MY WAY OF GIVING / COUNTRY COMFORT / CUT ACROSS SHORTY / LADY DAY / JO'S LAMENT / I DON'T WANT TO DISCUSS IT.

In Nick Logan and Bob Woffinden's *New Musical Express Encyclopedia Of Rock*, **Gasoline Alley** is described as 'arguably his finest album'. This viewpoint together with the general critical acclaim, particularly in America, eventually led to Mercury releasing this album together with **An Old Raincoat Won't Ever Let You Down** in 1976 as a double-package. Certainly this album was to establish Stewart in the U.S.A. as a solo singer. Stewart professed admiration for Martin Quittenton's arrangements, 'he's got such beautiful chords in his head' and also singled out the musicianship of Ron Wood and Micky Waller.

Rod used The Faces as backing musicians, though a line beneath the crediting of Wood, Lane, Jones said 'Mac not available due to a bus strike'. With a selection of ballads and much use of acoustic guitar, the songs on the album were markedly different from Faces' material. Stewart had three criteria for choosing his solo material. He looked for good songs which had not realised their chart potential; for material which he could adapt for his voice; and for basic melodies which he, himself, liked. So this album included his interpretation of the Elton John/Bernie Taupin composition, 'Country Comfort', from Elton John's **Tumbleweed Connection** album. There was a Steve Marriott/Ronnie Lane number, 'My Way Of Giving', which was recorded on The Small Faces' album, **From The Beginning**; Dylan's 'Only A Hobo', Bobby and Shirley Womack's 'It's All Over Now'. Stewart also added two excellent songs of his own, 'Lady Day' and 'Jo's Lament' plus the title track written with Rod Wood, 'Gasoline Alley'.

Stewart has always loved **Gasoline Alley**, for 'its complete naiveness', plus the wide variety of source material. Critics have liked the perfect way in which the musical variety blended. Conversations about the exact location of Gasoline Alley took place between Rod and interviewers from various musical papers. Rod said that the phrase came from an American girl he had met. His own Gasoline Alley was Highgate, or at least, this was said to the interviewer of *Zig Zag* magazine. However the album's cover has more in common with the song 'Only A Hobo' than Rod's home location which is a fairly affluent residential area of London.

Centre: In 1975 Rod held a press conference in Ireland for the release of **Atlantic Crossing** which included the hit single **Sailing**.

78

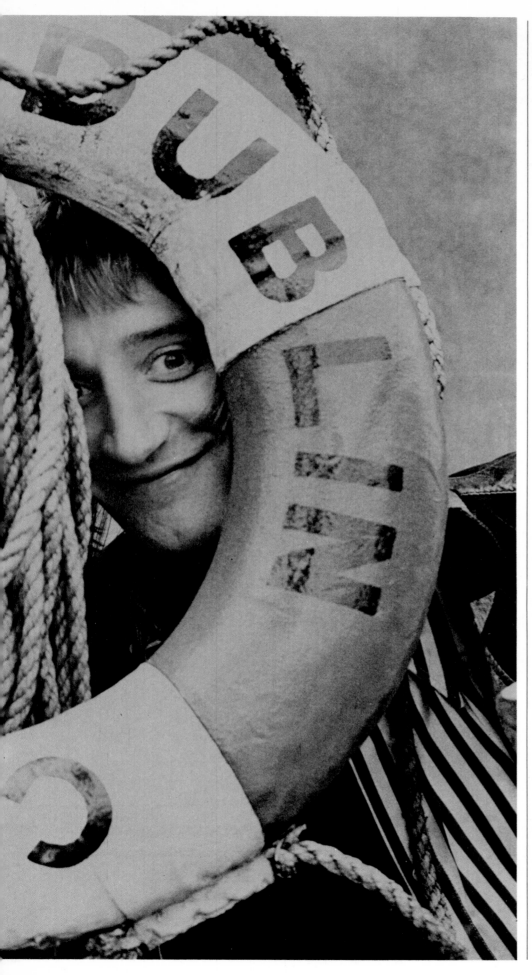

Every Picture Tells A Story (1971, Mercury) tracks:
EVERY PICTURE TELLS A STORY / SEEMS LIKE A LONG TIME / THAT'S ALL RIGHT / TOMORROW IS A LONG TIME / MAGGIE MAY / MANDOLIN WIND / (I KNOW) I'M LOSING YOU / REASON TO BELIEVE.

This superb album established Rod as a superstar. When he planned his third album, he wanted to make another **Gasoline Alley**. It didn't turn out that way, though his method of selecting material remained the same. Dylan provided him with 'Tomorrow Is A Long Time'; he chose a soul number '(I Know) I'm Losing You'; American singer, Tim Hardin, was the source of the moving 'Reason To Believe'. One of his most interesting selections was his choice and rendering of 'That's All Right', a number immortalized by Elvis Presley. Rod as both singer and producer chose excellent artists for vocal backing. He introduced the female voices of Maggie Bell, Doris Troy and Madeline Bell. Maggie was singled out for the descriptive words 'Mateus Rose Maggie Bell'. In interviews with magazines about the album, Stewart suggested that Maggie, the Scottish girl, who had been long associated with the talented Stone The Crows, would be well capable of making an outstanding album. He praised her vocal control and saw her as a cross between himself and Paul Rodgers of Free.

Rod's musicians also included Ron Wood, the talented Martin Quittenton (with whom he is credited as co-writer of the outstanding cut, 'Maggie May') and Ian McLagan. Piano and guitar accompaniment came from two John Baldry band members. In this album, Stewart aimed for the effect which Dylan obtained on his **Blonde On Blonde** extravaganza, especially the track, 'Sad Eyed Lady Of The Lowlands'. 'Mandolin Wind' has been chosen by Rod as his own favourite track, with splendid mandolin playing from Lindisfarne musician, Ray Jackson.

Every Picture Tells A Story rapidly soared to number five on its second week in the British charts and established Rod's success. He himself approached this success with some caution and reminded everyone that he had spent long enough aiming for this big moment of his life. He told *Record Mirror*'s, Bill McAllister, 'I think I had about given up hope of ever getting through in England because after the first two albums didn't mean much I thought it was all down to America, and maybe Europe'.

Never A Dull Moment (1972, Mercury) tracks:
TRUE BLUE / LOST PARAGUAYOS / MAMA YOU BEEN ON MY MIND / ITALIAN GIRLS / ANGEL / INTERLUDINGS / YOU WEAR IT WELL / I'D RATHER GO BLIND / TWISTIN' THE NIGHT AWAY.

For his fourth album, **Never A Dull Moment**, Rod chose tracks which were more in the style of The Faces. The opening album track, 'True Blue' had been recorded at the sessions from which came The Faces' **Ooh La La** album. Rod also selected Dylan's 'Mama You Been On My Mind', Sam Cooke's 'Twistin' The Night Away' and 'Angel'

by Jimi Hendrix. So, in contrast with former solo albums, here was Rod appearing to merge his two identities. Stewart later commented that he was pleased that the album's material could be used as material for Faces' concerts. Rod also told the music press that he wished to sell the album below the normal retail price. His recording company, however, did not agree with him!

Never A Dull Moment proved to be a good album but thought by some people not to compare with the previous two.

Sing It Again, Rod (1973, Mercury) tracks:
REASON TO BELIEVE / YOU WEAR IT WELL / MANDOLIN WIND / COUNTRY COMFORT / MAGGIE MAY / HANDBAGS AND GLADRAGS / STREET FIGHTING MAN / TWISTIN' THE NIGHT AWAY / LOST PARAGUAYOS / (I KNOW) I'M LOSING YOU / PINBALL WIZARD / GASOLINE ALLEY.

This was the only Stewart album to be issued in 1973. It was a compilation disc marketed by Mercury. The tracks were familiar, with the exception of an

interesting interpretation of 'Pinball Wizard' which Rod had sung in the stage production of Pete Townshend's **Tommy** in 1972.

Smiler (1974, Mercury) tracks:
SWEET LITTLE ROCK 'N' ROLLER / LOCHINVAR / FAREWELL / SAILOR / BRING IT ON HOME TO ME / YOU SEND ME / LET ME BE YOUR CAR / A NATURAL MAN / DIXIE TOOT / HARD ROAD / I'VE GROWN ACCUSTOMED TO HER FACE / GIRL FROM THE NORTH COUNTRY / MINE FOR ME.

Smiler was the last album which Rod recorded for Mercury. He moved to Warner Brothers and then to Riva. The album contained a fairly typical selection of songs. Apart from his own compositions with Quittenton and Wood, there was the usual Dylan number, 'Girl From The North Country', off the 1969, **Nashville Skyline** disc; Elton John's 'Let Me Be Your Car', (with E.J. playing piano and singing); McCartney's 'Mine For Me'; Sam Cooke's, 'Bring It On Home To Me'; the song, beautifully recorded by Aretha Franklin, '(You Make Me Feel Like) A Natural Man', (Aretha substituted 'woman'); Chuck Berry's, 'Sweet Little Rock 'n' Roller' and an instrumental version of 'I've Grown Accustomed To Her Face'. Stewart, during an interview, suggested that he might be singing that kind of material in the future. He said he enjoyed a wide variety of music and had a soft spot for good show music

SMILER

– in this case the music was from **My Fair Lady**. The traditional jazz band of Chris Barber backed the Stewart–Wood composition, 'Dixie Toot'. Rod performed this variety of songs with great skill and gave practical evidence of the remark, that he could sing 'anything, virtually everything'. The Sam Cooke songs became firm favourites at Faces' concerts. After the album, people close to Stewart wondered whether the life-style which Rod now enjoyed, might remove his past 'earthy' quality. Some critics of **Smiler** said that, apart from his own splendid song 'Farewell', the rest of the material seemed rather ordinary. Perhaps Rod sensed that people were largely unappreciative of this disc for he immediately made the decision to record his next album in America at Muscle Shoals Sound with the famous producer Tom Dowd. Among his backing musicians featured the renowned Steve Cropper.

Atlantic Crossing (1975, Warner Brothers) tracks:

I DON'T WANT TO TALK ABOUT IT / IT'S NOT THE SPOTLIGHT / THIS OLD HEART OF MINE / STILL LOVE YOU / SAILING / THREE TIME LOSER / ALRIGHT FOR AN HOUR / ALL IN THE NAME OF ROCK 'N' ROLL / DRIFT AWAY / STONE COLD SOBER.

Rod had again struck gold with **Atlantic Crossing** but it is doubtful whether he agreed with critics who said that this disc was the 'nadir' of his solo work so far. It was said that it was a technically perfect disc, the arrangements were immaculate but where was the Stewart 'soul'? The reviews of **Atlantic Crossing** were scattered with comparisons of a so-called 'working class kid' who had now gone to live with the show-biz Hollywood crowd and consequently lost 'real' music. Stewart, however, said that he had aimed for a more polished sound and a rhythm section which he felt he could get into.

This was the first solo disc made without Ron Wood and Mickey Waller. Rod sang more of his own songs and there were no Dylan tracks. There were plans for him to record with the Sutherland Brothers and Quiver but this did

not happen. Rod did include on the album, 'Sailing', a song which twice became a massive hit in Britain. The second release became a hit because 'Sailing' was chosen as the theme music for a T.V. series, and consequently brought Stewart's name into a 'family' context. At the press conference for the release of **Atlantic Crossing** Stewart said that he wished to create on stage the kind of sound he had on **Atlantic Crossing**. At this time there seemed a definite possibility that the band would break up. Later, in the music paper, *New Musical Express*, Ian McLagan described the album as 'sterile, un-emotional . . . he wasn't stretching him-self. I didn't like Sailing. It's pandering to the football crowds'.

A Night On The Town (1976, Riva) tracks:
THE BALL TRAP / PRETTY FLAMINGO / BIG BAYOU / THE WILD SIDE OF LIFE / TRADE WINDS / TONIGHT'S THE NIGHT / FIRST CUT IS THE DEEPEST / FOOL FOR YOU / THE KILLING OF GEORGIE. (1 & 2)

On this album where Stewart is now no longer a member of The Faces, he clearly shows his individuality. On the album cover he was portrayed in a Renoir-style painting on the front, and he was photographed wearing blazer, white shirt, black scarf and boater and holding a glass of champagne on the reverse. Only inside, on the cardboard sleeve which held the disc, did he look like the Rod of earlier days. Tom Dowd produced the album and the sources of song material were curtly credited 'All selections written or selected by R.S.' Rod wrote four of the nine album tracks. His best song was 'The Killing of Georgie', a memorable saga involving the death of a New York homosexual. **A Night On The Town** had a much better flow than **Atlantic Crossing**, being more spirited in its basic musical concept. This was partly due to Rod's choice of musicians. One of these was Chuck Berry's guitarist, Billy Peek. Apart from 'The Killing Of Georgie', the album supplied another major hit in 'Tonight's The Night'. This disc was played somewhat sparingly on European radio and television stations owing to phrases in the song, which described a girl losing her virginity.

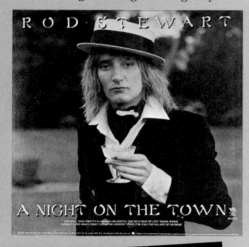

Recorded Action Highlights And Action Replays (1976, Phillips) tracks: CUT ACROSS SHORTY / BLIND PRAYER / ONLY A HOBO / OH NO NOT MY BABY / WHAT MADE MILWAUKEE FAMOUS (HAS MADE A LOSER OUT OF ME) / AN OLD RAINCOAT WON'T EVER LET YOU DOWN / ANGEL / CINDY'S LAMENT / LADY DAY / JO'S LAMENT / MY WAY OF GIVING / IT'S ALL OVER NOW.

This was another compilation album using recordings which Stewart made with the Mercury Record company.

The Vintage Years – 1969/1970 (1976, Mercury). A double album set of **An Old Raincoat Won't Ever Let You Down** and **Gasoline Alley**.

When this two-record set was released in Britain in March, 1976, this reminder of early Stewart days made many people aware of how the singer had changed over the years. The *New Musical Express* devoted most of its

Far left: Rod receives an award for the album **Every Picture Tells A Story** from Erwin Steinberg, president of Mercury Records. **Left:** Two personalities who contributed to Rod's success: Joe Smith, (left) president of Warners and Billy Gaff (right) Stewart's manager and director of Riva Records.

page 23, April 3, 1976, to a re-appraisal of these early works by Steve Clarke.

Clarke felt that all the tracks on both these albums were successful. Listening to these cuts also made Clarke wish once more for The Faces and ended his comment with the words, 'Honestly he ain't that good a singer in technical terms, but given the right situation can put a lot of his own feeling into something. And most of us (I think) wonder whether he's in the right situation now to continue making great music.' Doubtless though, there are those who wonder what all the fuss is about for, to them, Stewart remains tops.

The Best Of Rod Stewart. Volume 1. (1976, Mercury. U.S.A. only) tracks: MAGGIE MAY / CUT CROSS SHORTY / AN OLD RAINCOAT WON'T EVER LET YOU DOWN / I'M LOSING YOU / HANDBAGS AND GLADRAGS / IT'S ALL OVER NOW / STREET FIGHTING MAN / GASOLINE ALLEY / EVERY PICTURE TELLS A STORY / WHAT MADE MILWAUKEE FAMOUS / OH NO NOT MY BABY / JODIE / YOU WEAR IT WELL / LET ME BE YOUR CAR /PINBALL WIZARD / SAILOR / ANGEL / MINE FOR ME.

The Best Of Rod Stewart. Volume 2. (1976, Mercury, U.S.A. only) tracks: MAN OF CONSTANT SORROW / BLIND PRAYER / LONG DAY / TOMORROW IS A LONG TIME / COUNTRY COMFORTS / MANDOLIN WIND / THAT'S ALL RIGHT / MY WAY OF GIVING / I DON'T WANT TO DISCUSS IT / REASON TO BELIEVE / ITALIAN GIRLS / I'D RATHER GO BLIND / LOST PARAGUAYOS / TRUE BLUE / SWEET LITTLE ROCK 'N' ROLLER / HARD ROAD / YOU MAKE ME FEEL LIKE A NATURAL MAN / BRING IT ON HOME TO ME / YOU SEND ME / TWISTIN' THE NIGHT AWAY.

A Shot Of Rhythm And Blues (1977, Private Stock. U.S.A. only).
This album, containing songs recorded between 1964 and 1966, was the subject of legal battle between those representing Rod Stewart and the recording company, whilst this volume was being prepared. Rod Stewart claimed that the tracks were intended for demonstration purposes only. It was feared that the album's sleeve design would give the impression of it being an up-to-date Stewart recording. *Rolling Stone* reviewer, Dave Marsh comments '**A Shot of Rhythm and Blues** is so blatantly exploitative that even a Rod Stewart fanatic like myself feels embarrassed by its release.'

Other Rod Stewart album tracks:
With Steampacket. **Rock Generation Vol. 6.** 1971. (Released in France with label number, BYG 529 706) track: 'Can I Get A Witness'. With others of the cast of **Tommy – A Rock Opera.** (1972, Ode SP 9901) track: 'Pinball Wizard'.

With Denis Law, **Scotland Scotland**, track: 'Angel' (1974, Polydor).

This Picture Tells A Story – Rod's Success.

Undoubtedly Rod Stewart has come a long way from his early days of simple verse in the Jeff Beck era, to the forceful words which describe the 'Killing Of Georgie'. Though, perhaps, it is true to say there were 'ups' and 'downs' in the intervening period of time, rather than a steady progress.

When Stewart commented upon his lyrics on the album, **Beck Ola**, taking one song in particular, 'Hangman's Knee', he called it 'really stupid'. His first solo album, **An Old Raincoat Won't Ever Let You Down** suggested more the process, which continued on future albums, of Stewart's ability to choose a good, and often little known, song which suited his singing and vocal range. By the second album, Stewart's music was more polished and his lyrics sharper. Two of his songs in particular caught the attention of most people, 'Lady Day' and its following album cut, 'Jo's Lament'. 'Jo's Lament' clearly showed one important aspect of Stewart's writing. He was at his best when describing situations or people he knew from first-hand experience.

Stewart wrote much of his best album material with either Ron Wood or Martin Quittenton. With Wood, he wrote songs for The Faces, as well as material designated for solo work. He and Wood wrote songs which they knew that their Faces' audiences would enjoy. For instance the song, 'That's All You Need' (on **A Nod's As Good As A Wink**) which talked of someone's violin-playing brother who thought intelligence was everything but eventually discovered that music was just that.

Stewart, early in his solo career, said that he wrote words which rhymed. When working with Martin Quittenton, he would call him on the phone and say that he had some song ideas. The two would get together and Quittenton would usually respond to the kind of tempo which Stewart had in mind and suggest particular riffs. Eventually the two would come up with a more-or-less completed song. It was this partnership which produced such good songs as 'Farewell', 'Maggie May', and the big single hit, 'You Wear It Well'.

Rod Stewart says little about his writing, and when he does, it seems he often plays down this side of his talent. He has called writing a 'hard slog' and has said that he doesn't have too much to say. He once told Britain's *Beat Instrumental* that writers must surely be people brimming with ideas and thoughts and that his only forte was his memory and experiences. Stewart has said that performing is 'where it's at'. Since his tour which began in late 1976, critics and interviewers in the broadcasting media have begun to suggest that we should pay more attention to Rod Stewart the songwriter.

ROD'S
CAREER CALENDAR

1945 On January 10 Roderick David Stewart is born in London's Highgate, the fifth child to Bob and Elsie Stewart.

1956 He attends the William Grimshaw school in Hornsey. He is a prefect and plays in the school first XI soccer team. He has ideas of becoming a professional football player.

1961 Easter sees Rod joining the Aldermaston marchers who are supporting the Campaign for Nuclear Disarmament. Later in the year, Rod signs professional forms with Brentford Football Club. He is paid £8 a week, (then around 20 U.S. dollars).

1962 The Aldermaston March becomes an annual event and Rod is amongst the marchers in 1962. He spends his summer travelling around Europe and he is arrested in St Tropez for vagrancy.

1963 Rod again walks with the Aldermaston marchers. He gets his first musical break with the Dimensions, a rhythm and blues group. He blows harmonica and has occasional opportunities to sing. The band is hired to back vocalist Jimmy Powell, who eventually takes over the harmonica playing.

1964 Cyril Davies, co-lead vocalist with Long John Baldry in the R&B All Stars, dies at the age of 32. Baldry forms the Hoochie Coochie Men and Rod joins as a vocalist. Early summer sees Rod making his first recording He duets with Baldry on the song, **Up Above My Head**, the B-side of Baldry's single for United Artists, **You'll Be Mine**. Rod receives no label credits. In October, the first single under Rod's own name appears, **Good Morning Little Schoolgirl**. The Yardbirds make a competing version. Rod makes his first solo television performance on a British pop show, **Ready Steady Go!** Hoochie Coochie Men break up and Rod plays dates with the Soul Agents.

1965 In April, Rod joins a new band, Steam Packet. The band go on a short, early-summer tour with The Rolling Stones and the Walker Brothers. Near the end of the year, Rod is featured in a 30 minute TV documentary, **Rod The Mod**. Steam Packet make a couple of rough tapes. These do not appear until 1971, on the French BYG label. Another Stewart single is issued, **The Day Will Come**.

1966 Early in the year, British EMI issue **Shake**, Rod's version of a Sam Cooke song. Rod leaves Steam Packet in March and the band splits up after their summer St Tropez engagement. Rod joins Shotgun Express and makes one single with the group, **I Could Feel The Whole World Turn Round**, for Columbia. In December, Rod joins The Jeff Beck Group. Ron Wood, previously with The Birds, also joins. On December 11, Jeff Beck is reported signing a solo recording contract with producer, Mickie Most.

1967 The first single is released by the Jeff Beck Group but Beck sings lead on **Hi Ho Silver Lining** and Rod does not feature on the disc. The group commence their first tour of Britain in March, billed with The Small Faces. Their first night, at London's Finsbury Park Astoria, is a failure and they leave the tour. In August the Jeff Beck group meet The Small Faces again for the National Rhythm and Blues Festival at Windsor, England. Rod sings on the B-side of the next Jeff Beck Group single, **Tallyman**.

1968 The Jeff Beck Group release an instrumental version of **Love Is Blue**. Rod sings on the B-side, **I've Been Drinking**. On May 28, Rod flies with the band to the U.S.A. for their eight-week tour. The tour is very successful and they draw large crowds. The band's first album, **Truth** is released in the U.S.A. and in Britain later in the year. Three songs are credited to Rod on the album sleeve. In October Rod signs a solo recording contract with American producer, Lou Reizner of Mercury Records.

1969 The Jeff Beck Group fly back to America and in January they appear at Fillmore East, New York. A second album, **Beck Ola** is released. Rod becomes increasingly more successful as a vocalist. A split is imminent, however, and Beck plans to form a new group with Rod, Tim Bogart from Vanilla Fudge and Carmine Appice. In June, a single from the album, **Beck Ola** is released: **Plynth (Water Down The Drain)**. Steve Marriott leaves The Small Faces and Ron Wood is rumoured as his replacement. Rod makes one appearance with The Small Faces at a Cambridge gig. Later there are reports of the Small Faces changing their name to The Faces and of Rod joining the newly named band as lead singer. Mercury Records agree that Rod could record for The Small Faces. At the same time, the group leave the Immediate record label and sign with Warner Brothers.

Top Left: Long John Baldry. **Centre:** Rod Stewart's first appearance on BBC TV's Top Of The Pops. **Below:** Record producer Lou Reizner of Mercury who signed Stewart for solo recordings in October 1968. **Right:** Face to Face.

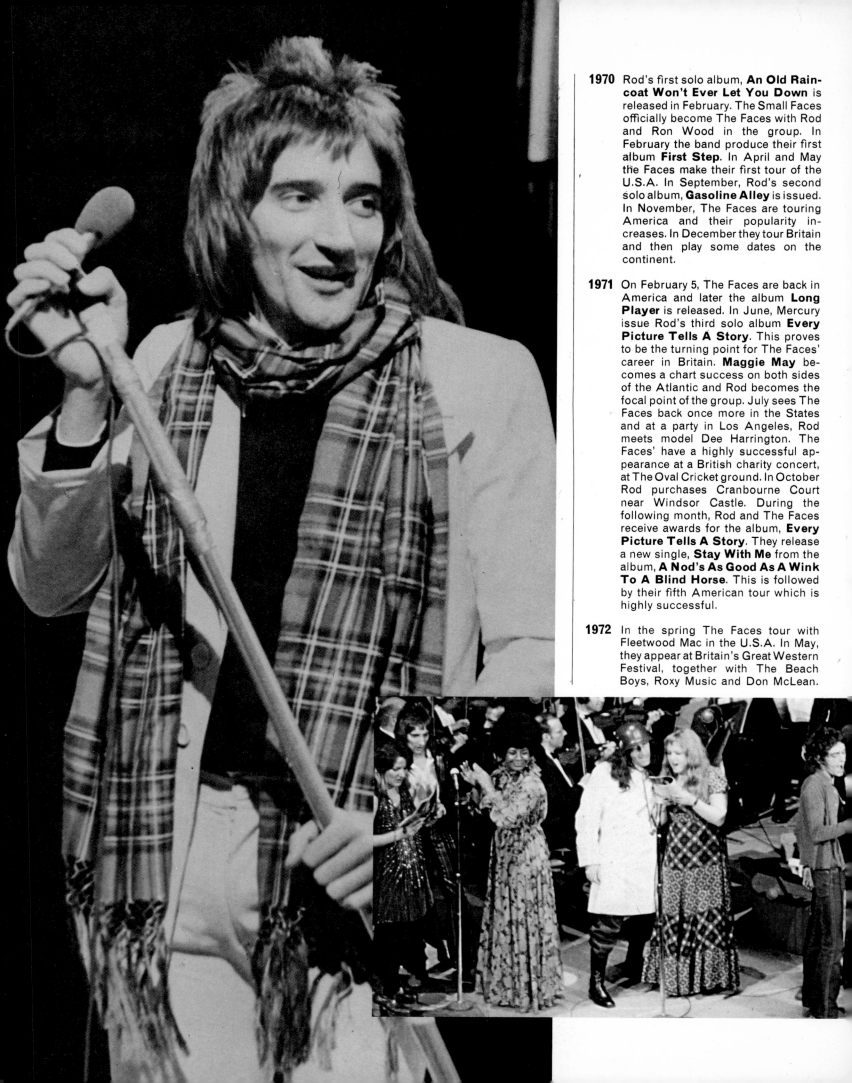

1970 Rod's first solo album, **An Old Raincoat Won't Ever Let You Down** is released in February. The Small Faces officially become The Faces with Rod and Ron Wood in the group. In February the band produce their first album **First Step**. In April and May the Faces make their first tour of the U.S.A. In September, Rod's second solo album, **Gasoline Alley** is issued. In November, The Faces are touring America and their popularity increases. In December they tour Britain and then play some dates on the continent.

1971 On February 5, The Faces are back in America and later the album **Long Player** is released. In June, Mercury issue Rod's third solo album **Every Picture Tells A Story**. This proves to be the turning point for The Faces' career in Britain. **Maggie May** becomes a chart success on both sides of the Atlantic and Rod becomes the focal point of the group. July sees The Faces back once more in the States and at a party in Los Angeles, Rod meets model Dee Harrington. The Faces' have a highly successful appearance at a British charity concert, at The Oval Cricket ground. In October Rod purchases Cranbourne Court near Windsor Castle. During the following month, Rod and The Faces receive awards for the album, **Every Picture Tells A Story**. They release a new single, **Stay With Me** from the album, **A Nod's As Good As A Wink To A Blind Horse**. This is followed by their fifth American tour which is highly successful.

1972 In the spring The Faces tour with Fleetwood Mac in the U.S.A. In May, they appear at Britain's Great Western Festival, together with The Beach Boys, Roxy Music and Don McLean.

In July, Rod's fourth album, **Never A Dull Moment** is released. Rod again enters the British charts with **In A Broken Dream**, a song recorded with Python Lee Jackson. Mercury issue the single **Angel** from **Never A Dull Moment** during November. In December Rod appears in the London stage production of Pete Townshend's rock opera **Tommy**, singing **Pinball Wizard**.

1973 The Faces release **Cindy Incidentally**, their first single for over a year. A new album is released in April titled **Ooh La La**. During April and May, The Faces are once more in America. They return at the end of May and member Ronnie Lane announces that he is leaving the band. Rod has a compilation album issued by Mercury during July titled **Sing It Again, Rod**. The previously cancelled European tour takes place from July 16 to 29, with Japanese musician, Tetsu Yamauchi, making his first appearance. At a Manchester gig, Faces drummer, Kenny Jones collapses but later recovers. Mercury issue another single recorded by Rod, **Oh No, Not My Baby**. On September 12, The Faces leave for America. On their return to Britain, Warner Brothers release The Faces' single **Pool Hall Richard**, and the band tour Britain in December. A live album recorded in California, **Coast To Coast Overture And Beginners**, was released credited as Rod Stewart and The Faces.

In January The Faces leave for Australia and New Zealand. On their return, they play some British dates which extend into February. Warner Brothers issue some of The Faces' best-known songs in June on a maxi-single and The band play at Buxton

Festival. In July, Ron Wood plays with an assortment of musicians, including Keith Richard, at a London concert. In August, The Faces fly to America for a Festival. Ron Wood records and promotes his solo album. In September The Faces start a tour of Europe which lasts almost four months. This tour proves to be a huge success. In September both Rod's **Smiler** album and Ron Wood's **I've Got My Own Album To Do** are released. Kenny Jones has a single issued in October but has no plans for a solo career. Mid-November sees the release of The Faces single with one of the longest titles in the history of pop, **You Can Make Me Dance, Sing Or Anything (Even Take The Dog For A Walk, Mend A Fuse, Fold Away The Ironing Board, Or Any Other Domestic Shortcomings)**. The single coincides with the British appearances on their European tour. Paul and Linda McCartney attend the concert, at Lewisham, London, and join Rod on stage. Paul had written a song for Rod titled, **Mine For Me**, which appears on **Smiler**. Elton John attends several concerts together with many other stars and celebrities.

1975 Rod and The Faces begin recording a new album but the band have an American tour in February and March. They book time at a studio in Los Angeles but things go astray as Ron and Rod have their solo activities very much in mind. In March Rod meets Britt Eckland, and the same month sees him attending the Grammy Awards dinner. Rod takes a lease on a flat in Belgravia, London. In April, Rod leaves for American recording sessions and he says he will live permanently in the States. In June, Ron Wood becomes a temporary member

of the Rolling Stones. In British musical papers during July, Kenny Jones voices his dissatisfaction with the progress of The Faces. There are reports of Rod Stewart owing British tax amounting to £750,000. In August, a new single, **Sailing** is released by Warner Brothers with **Stone Cold Sober** on the B-side. Rod flies with Britt to Ireland and there, he holds a press conference to promote his new album, **Atlantic Crossing**. Another tour of the States is announced which begins on August 15. It takes in 35 cities and after America, there are performances arranged for Japan, Australia, New Zealand and Europe. The band begins to show signs of splitting up and in December Rod announces his intention of leaving The Faces.

1976 Warner Brothers refuse to provide financial backing for a new Faces' album unless a tour could be arranged. This did not prove to be possible and the Faces finally split up. Rod has a succession of single hits including the **Killing Of Georgie (Parts I and II)**, and **Tonight's The Night** and he tops charts on both sides of the Atlantic. **Sailing** becomes the signature tune of a BBC TV programme. Rod's version of the Lennon-McCartney hit **Get Back** is featured in the Lou Reizner film, **World War II**. A new Rod Stewart album, **A Night On The Town** is issued. A BBC TV documentary is made featuring Rod with Britt Eckland. Rod forms his own band and tours are drawn up for Britain, Europe and the U.S.A. with, what is termed a World Tour, commencing in Norway, on October 30. Rod plays in London before Christmas and is televised by the BBC for national viewing. Rod spends Christmas in Britain.

1977 In January, Rod flies from Britain with the band for the remainder of their World Tour. Some members of the band's road crew were arrested by Scottish police for alleged possession of drugs. Private Stock Records in U.S.A. issue an album comprising recordings made between 1964–66 as demo tapes which results in Rod suing the company. Early summer sees the release of a new album, **The Best Of The Faces**, in the U.K.

Left: The cast of the rock opera Tommy written by Pete Townshend of the Who. Rod, who sang **Pinball Wizard**, is seen standing on the far left.

ACKNOWLEDGMENTS

The publishers would like to thank the following individuals and organizations for their kind permission to reproduce the photographs in this book:

BBC Photograph Library 68, Andre Csillag 4–5, 8–9, 36, 70 inset, 81; Dagmar endpapers, 6–7, 38–39; Ian Dickson 53; David W Ellis 84–85; Robert Ellis 18–19, 22 above, 24 above, 25, 27, 28–29, 32 left, 32–33, 34–35, 43 above, 43 below left, 50 below, 54, 54–55, 55, 78–79, 86–87, 90–91; London Features International (Henry Diltz) 76–77, (Sam Emerson) 45, (Mike Putland) 20, 24–25 below, 26, 88–89; National Playing Fields Association 71 inset; Rex Features Ltd. 14 below right, 43 below right, 60 left, 63, (Dezo Hoffmann Ltd.) 12–13, 13 right, 21 above, (Feri Lukas) 14 below centre; Scope Features 58–59, (Allan Ballard) 60 right, (David Steen) 48–49, 56–57, 61, 62–63, 64–65, 64 inset, 69, 70–71; SKR Photos International Ltd. 10–11, 12 left, 14 below left, 14–15, 16–17, 23 inset, 62 inset, 65 inset, 88 above left, centre left and below left, 90, 92–93; Chris Walter (Photo Features International) 29, 34.